Show it off!

Designing Scrapbook Pages and Projects for Display

From the Editors of Memory Makers Books

Memory Makers Books
Cincinnati, Ohio
www.memorymakersmagazine.com

MEMORY
MAKERS
BOOKS

Show it off! Copyright© 2008 by Memory Makers Books. Manufactured in China. All rights reserved. It is permissible for the purchaser to make the projects contained herein and sell them at fairs, bazaars and craft shows. No other part of this book may be reproduced in any form or by any electronic or mechanical means including information storage and retrieval systems without permission in writing from the publisher, except by a reviewer, who may quote a brief passage in review. Published by Memory Makers Books, an imprint of F+W Publications, Inc., 4700 East Galbraith Road, Cincinnati, Ohio 45236. (800) 289-0963. First edition.

12 11 10 09 08   5 4 3 2 1

Distributed in Canada by Fraser Direct
100 Armstrong Avenue
Georgetown, ON, Canada L7G 5S4
Tel: (905) 877-4411

Distributed in the U.K. and Europe by David & Charles
Brunel House, Newton Abbot, Devon, TQ12 4PU, England
Tel: (+44) 1626 323200, Fax: (+44) 1626 323319
E-mail: postmaster@davidandcharles.co.uk

Distributed in Australia by Capricorn Link
P.O. Box 704, S. Windsor, NSW 2756 Australia
Tel: (02) 4577-3555

Library of Congress Cataloging-in-Publication Data
Show it off! : designing scrapbook pages and projects for display / editors of Memory Makers Books. -- 1st ed.
    p. cm.
  Includes index.
  ISBN 978-1-59963-025-0 (pbk. : alk. paper)
  1. Photograph albums. 2. Scrapbooks. 3. Memory in art. I. Memory Makers Books.
TR501.S535 2008
745.593--dc22
                    2007043494

fw
F+W PUBLICATIONS, INC.

www.fwpublications.com

Editor *Kristin Belsher*
Designer *Kelly O'Dell*
Art Coordinator *Eileen Aber*
Production Coordinator *Matt Wagner*
Photographers *Tim Grondin*
                Al Parrish
                Christine Polomsky
Stylist *Jan Nickum*
Writer *Torrey Scott*

Contributing Artists

Jodi Amidei

Vicki Boutin

Catherine Feegel-Erhardt

Cari Fennell

Amy Goldstein

Alecia Ackerman Grimm

Greta Hammond

Barb Hogan

Nic Howard

Vanessa Hudson

Gretchen McElveen

Sandi Minchuk

Amy Peterman

Suzy Plantamura

Mou Saha

Torrey Scott

Genevieve Simmonds

Cindy Smith

Kathleen Summers

Tiffany Tillman

Christine Traversa

Sarah van Wijck

Samantha Walker

Courtney Walsh

Tania Willis

Introduction

Over the years, scrapbooking has grown and evolved into more than just a hobby. Today, scrapbookers are artists, elevating scrapbooking from a hobby to an art form. And memory art has found its niche in the art world. It's the next rung on the evolutionary ladder of scrapbooking, and allows us, as scrapbookers, to spread our creative wings and take that giant leap from two dimensional to 3-D.

Memory art is a multi-media art form that is well suited for display on walls, tabletops, bookshelves, even in jewelry. Not only is it versatile, it's fun! The beauty of memory art is that, unlike traditional scrapbooking, there are no rules! Memory art is all about playing and experimenting. Let's face it, before memory art, we were limited to the depth and dimension we could add to a layout. After all, layouts get squished under a page protector; and when this happens, a great deal of a page's dimensional appeal gets smashed as well. Memory art gives us the freedom to expand the flat boundaries we often find ourselves trapped in.

Although creating dimensional scrapbook pieces can seem a daunting task, we promise that the more you let go, the easier and more comfortable it gets! Though we will never completely let go of our love of albums layouts, it's nice to know we have some dimensional choices when it comes to our creative outlets. So, take a deep breath, grab some lumpy stuff and start playing! There is creative freedom in lumpiness. It's time to break free of the album and show it off!

Creating Layouts
FOR
DISPLAY

It seems a shame to lock our favorite layouts away in the dark recesses of an album, just to be taken out and shared once in a blue moon. These layouts deserve more. Wouldn't it be great if they could break free of their bindings and grace our homes so that we could enjoy them all the time? Well, why not? We're about to show you how to take flat layouts, and with a little tweaking, a bit of inspiration and a dash of daring, transform them into display art. It's simple, and it's fun! You'll be amazed at how easy it is to let your creative juices flow. Come on! It's time to turn flat into fabulous.

Although patterned papers can give the illusion of dimension, sometimes there's just no substitute for the real McCoy. Vicki was able to convey dimension in her original layout while keeping it pancake-flat. But watch as her layout spreads its dimensional wings when she turns it loose to fly! The paper accents take flight in this layout for the wall. All it takes is some adhesive foam, a sprinkling of buttons and lots of layers.

Acrylic Frame

Supplies: Acrylic frame (Pageframe); cardstock; patterned paper (Heidi Grace); buttons (Autumn Leaves); butterfly template, stamps (Fiskars); ink; rub-on (Scenic Route); rhinestones; ribbon (unknown); pen

Princess Vicki Boutin

Supplies: Cardstock; glittery stickers, patterned paper (Heidi Grace); buttons (Autumn Leaves); butterfly template, stamps (Fiskars); ink; rub-on (Scenic Route); pen

Plastic Board

Supplies: Storyboard layout (Adobe); digital elements (ScrapArtist); mounted on Styrene (photo lab)

It's easy to incorporate multiple photos on a scrapbook layout. We do it all the time! That's old news to us seasoned scrapbookers. But how can we include lots of photos in our memory art without it looking segmented or cluttered? Amy shows us how successfully it can be done. She digitally merged several photos into a montage and superimposed a translucent title. It all comes together in an eye-catching design that looks great on the wall. Three cheers for image editing software!

Superstar Amy Goldstein   Supplies: Digital elements and paper (ScrapArtist); Impact, Myriad fonts (Microsoft)

Aaaah, vacation. The smell of suntan lotion, the sound of the waves on the beach, the warmth of the sun. Part of vacation is gathering souvenirs. Some souvenirs, like paper ephemera, can easily be included in a flat layout. Others, like seashells, trinkets and other treasures, are not so easy. Alecia was able to maintain her original layout concept while including all those fun keepsakes by placing everything in a shadow box.

Shadow Box

Supplies: Shadow box (Target); patterned paper (Adornit, American Crafts, Creative Imaginations, Die Cuts With A View, Flair Designs, KI Memories); mesh (Magic Mesh); chipboard words (unknown); number stickers (KI Memories); label maker (Around the Block); ribbon (Rusty Pickle, SEI); stickers (K&Co.); beads, shell (Mermaid Tears); sequins; ink

Supplies: Patterned paper (Adornit, American Crafts, Die Cuts With A View, Flair Designs, KI Memories); chipboard words (unknown); number stickers (KI Memories); label maker (Around the Block); glitter; mesh (Magic Mesh); ink

Our Beach Vacation Alecia Ackerman Grimm

Some layouts are pretty as a picture just as they are. All that's needed to take them out of the album and onto the wall is a frame. But frames can be boring. Greta took care of this in no time flat by moving her decorative elements off the layout and overlapping them on the frame. She also took a plain-Jane unfinished wood frame and, using acrylic paints and crackle medium, turned it into the perfect border to showcase her layout.

Wood Frame

Supplies: Frame (unknown); patterned paper (Fancy Pants, K&Co.); chipboard, rub-on (Fancy Pants); buttons (Autumn Leaves); acrylic paint; crackle medium; lace (unknown); ink; Vivaldi font (Microsoft)

Showing It Off
What makes good display art?

- Projects with big, oversized photos.

- Single-subject photos. They make a stronger visual impact than a group of shots with a lot going on.

- Minimal or no journaling. If possible, use journaling solely as a decorative element.

- Creations with a strong, visible title.

- Bold page elements and backgrounds (like color blocking). These are more striking than finely detailed elements.

- When it comes to colors think bold, bright and vibrant. Dull colors fade into the background.

Supplies: Cardstock; patterned paper (Fancy Pants, K&Co.); chipboard, ribbon, rub-ons (Fancy Pants); buttons (Autumn Leaves); acrylic paint; lace (unknown); ink; Vivaldi font (Microsoft)

A Greta Hammond

Many of us would like to display our layouts in our homes. But cardstock and patterned paper are not sturdy enough for duties outside the album. Suzy was undaunted by this prospect. She modified her layout and fortified it with a chipboard and foam board foundation. This simple reinforcement is all that you need to safely display your layouts sans album.

Chipboard and Foam

Supplies: Cardstock; scalloped cardstock (Bazzill); chipboard letters (Maya Road); starfish and shells (Michaels); ribbon (unknown); foam; ink; pen

From Flat to Fabulous
How to create dimension

- You *can* create dimension using flat objects. The secret is layers. Separate layers of flat elements with adhesive foam.

- Attach found objects or memorabilia to layouts.

- Add dimensional embellishments like silk flowers, big buttons and metal ribbon slides.

- Experiment with dimensional media and techniques like modeling paste, embossing, decoupage and dimensional paint.

Supplies: Cardstock; patterned paper (Creative Imaginations); chipboard letters (Maya Road); buttons (Autumn Leaves); ribbon (unknown); ink; pen

Family Suzy Plantamura

Collage Frame

Supplies: Frame (Dennis Daniels); cardstock; chipboard letters (Scenic Route); stamps (Inque Boutique); ink; pen

Scrapbooking outside the album gives us license to pull out all the stops. Often, we limit ourselves to the amount of time and effort we put into the creation of our layouts. We use a lot of shortcuts. Pretty, pre-made embellishments, stickers, and die-cuts can be the "fast food" of our scrapbooking. When Kathleen decided to take her layout out of the album, she knew she wanted to give it a personal touch by illustrating her own embellishments. Memory art is the perfect recipe for letting out your inner "gourmet chef."

Supplies: Cardstock chipboard letters (Heidi Swapp, Scenic Route); stamps, ink (Inque Boutique); pen

Love Grows Kathleen Summers

Supplies: Chipboard; cardstock;
patterned paper, rub-on letters
(Karen Foster); rub-on swirls
(BasicGrey); acrylic paint; ink;
foam board; thread

Collage frames can be pricey, and
they limit you to whatever size and
number of openings are in the frame.
When Cindy wanted to take her
favorite multi-photo layout to the
wall, she decided that the best way
to accomplish this was to make her
own collage "frame" using foam
board. Foam board is a memory
artist's best friend. It's light, sturdy,
easy to work with, inexpensive and,
best of all, dimensional.

Foam Board

Supplies: Cardstock;
patterned paper, rub-on
letters (Karen Foster); rub-on
swirls (BasicGrey); ink; floss

Capture Life Cindy Smith

$\mathcal{S}$how me how! Making a Collage Frame

You will need | *foam board at least 12" x 16" (30cm x 41cm), acrylic paint, 12" x 12" (30cm x 30cm) sheet of cardstock, adhesive, sewing machine (optional), photos, scissors or paper trimmer, rub-ons, ink (optional), chipboard, picture hanger*

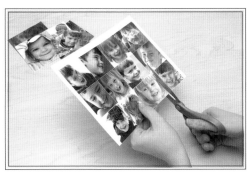

Cut one piece of foam board to 12" x 12" (30cm x 30cm). Cut three smaller squares to 3⅞" (10cm). Paint the front and sides of each foam board piece. Then attach the cardstock to the large piece of foam board. (If desired, stitch the borders of the cardstock before attaching it to the foam board.)

Cut three photos into 3⅞" (10cm) squares. Cut 11 photos into 1⅞" (5cm) squares. Cut a piece of patterned paper to 3⅞" x 1⅞" (10cm x 5cm) for your title. Add rub-on designs and letters to the title piece.

Attach the painted squares of foam board (from step 1) to the back of the three larger photos. Attach chipboard to the back of some of the smaller photos and the title block. Ink the edges of each square, if desired.

Assemble the squares on the foam board, leaving space between each photo so the finished piece resembles a collage frame. Then attach a picture hanger to the back of the foam board.

While detailed, heartfelt journaling is an important aspect of scrapbooking, sometimes it either doesn't fit or is just too personal to put on display. Not to worry. Samantha shows us how she uses her real journaling for the album layout and uses phrase stickers as embellishment on her memory art. As long as you have the important journaling somewhere (on a layout or on the back of your project), it's OK to exclude journaling from your memory art.

Frame

You just might be the cutest thing ever.

That smile just melts me.

Hey you cute little chickie.

YOU'RE A BLAST.   Sweet.

Love, love, love you.

YOU JUST MAKE ME SMILE KIDDO.

You are something special.

MY LITTLE LOVE.

I'm so crazy about you.

I adore you (always will).

YOU'RE THE SWEETEST.

I hope you know just how much I love you.

YOU...making this world a cuter place.

Yep, you're pretty darn cute.

More than all the stars in the sky...I love you.

All those girly little ways.

Yep, you're pretty darn cute.

Love you more every single day.

C U T I E · P I E.

Let me count the ways...

How did you get so sweet?

LITTLE WILD CHILD (ya, you):

SWEETHEART.

You are wonderful (lucky me).

You are beautiful (in sooooooooooooo many way

Supplies: Frame (unknown); cardstock; chipboard letters and flower, patterned paper, scroll and word stickers (Creative Imaginations); rickrack; ink

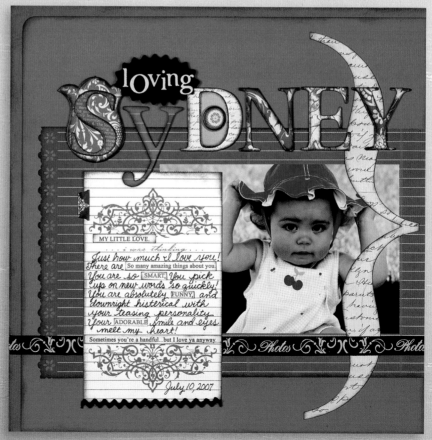

loving SYDNEY

MY LITTLE LOVE.

...i was thinking...

Just how much I love you! There are So many amazing things about you. You are so SMART. You pick up on new words so quickly! You are absolutely FUNNY, and downright historical with your teasing personality. Your ADORABLE smile and eyes melt my heart!

Sometimes you're a handful...but I love ya anyway.

July 10, 2007

Supplies: Cardstock; chipboard letters, patterned paper, ribbon, stickers (Creative Imaginations); letter stickers (Chatterbox); rickrack; ink; pen

Loving Sydney Samantha Walker

Window panes have the power to draw our attentions inward. They invite us to get a closer look, and beckon us to sneak a peek. Color blocking is an effective, easy and eye-catching way to create a layout with a window-pane look. And with memory art, we don't have to stop at paper blocks. A wooden window-pane frame is the perfect way to maintain a crisp, graphic look while creating a whole other world to peer into.

Collage Frame

Supplies: Frame (Hobby Lobby); die-cut flowers and tags, patterned paper (Daisy D's); brads; chipboard letter (Li'l Davis); label (Jenni Bowlin); epoxy words (Provo Craft); button (Autumn Leaves); ink

Supplies: Cardstock; button, die-cut flowers, patterned paper (Daisy D's); label (Jenni Bowlin); chipboard letter (Li'l Davis); epoxy words (Provo Craft); acrylic paint; ink; adhesive foam

I Heart You Tania Willis

What does it take to convert a layout into memory art? Sometimes it's just a subtle shift in the focus of the layout. In Amy's page you're drawn to the title and the journaling. The words tell the story. But in her on-the-wall version, the photos do the talking. Keeping the photos the same size and placing them in a horizontal series draws the viewer's eye across the creation like a picture book story.

Wood Frame

Supplies: Frame (handmade by artist); storyboard layout (Adobe); Carpenter ITG font (Internet download)

On Display
The ins and outs of creating a display around your memory art

- Use good lighting. Natural is better.

- If using artificial lighting, choose bulbs that show true colors. Avoid fluorescent and neon bulbs.

- If you're framing your work, choose a frame that complements your creation rather than competing with it.

- Memory art, including framed pieces, doesn't have to be displayed on the wall. Try other venues like coffee tabletops, desks, shelves, glass cabinets and doorknobs.

- Don't clutter up the display area with unrelated knickknacks.

- Try grouping a few creations together to make a display. Odd numbers are generally more appealing to the eye than even ones.

Anticipation Amy Goldstein

Supplies: Digital elements and papers (Jen Wilson); Myriad font (Microsoft)

There is no such thing as too much bling! Well, maybe when it comes to layouts there is. Let's face it, bling is lumpy; but some subjects just scream for bling. So what's the solution? Do what Catherine did. Find a fun and funky object, like this rhinestone-encrusted clock, that is the perfect accompaniment for those darling photos and turn it into memory art. Try altering a clock's face. It will look oh so fabulous, dah-ling.

Clock

Supplies: Clock (unknown); patterned paper (Anna Griffin); rub-ons, transparency (Hambly); rhinestones (Heidi Swapp); rickrack (All My Memories); ink

Supplies: Patterned paper (Anna Griffin); rub-ons, transparency (Hambly); rhinestones, transparent letters (Heidi Swapp); glitter glue; ribbon; tags; pin; adhesive foam; thread; pen

Believe Catherine Feegel-Erhardt

When we think of quintessential art that hangs on the wall, we often think in terms of canvas—stretched on a frame, then painted. This technique can be adapted easily from a scrapbook layout. Barb took the opportunity to add loads of texture to her hanging masterpiece by using modeling paste and a dimensional silk flower. Whether they end up propped on a tabletop, or hanging on the wall, stretched canvas creations give you, well, a blank canvas to work on when creating memory art.

Artist Canvas

Supplies: Artist canvas; cardstock; canvas paper (Marshalls); patterned paper, ribbon (7gypsies); brads, metal accent, paper flowers (Making Memories); modeling paste (Golden); paints; sunflower (Michaels); pen; digital elements by Anna Aspnes and Katie Pertiet (Designer Digitals); image editing software (Adobe)

Supplies: Cardstock; patterned paper, ribbon (7gypsies); brads, metal accent, paper flowers (Making Memories); thread; pen; digital elements by Anna Aspnes and Katie Pertiet (Designer Digitals); image editing software (Adobe)

Christmas Photo 2006 Barb Hogan

*S*how me how! Making a Textured Frame

You will need | *artist canvas square, pencil, painter's tape, modeling paste, palette knife or butter knife, acrylic paint (two colors), brush*

With a pencil, mark a 1" (3cm) border around the edges of the canvas square. Mark off the border with painter's tape. The tape should be placed 1" (3cm) from each edge of the canvas square.

Apply modeling paste to the canvas border with a small palette knife or butter knife. Spread the paste like you would frost a cake, creating ridges. Apply the modeling paste in thin layers to avoid cracking. Remove the painter's tape while the paste is still wet. Allow the modeling paste to set for 24 hours.

Apply acrylic paint to the canvas square making sure to completely cover the modeling paste. Allow the paint to dry. Apply a second color of acrylic paint with a dry brush to highlight the texture of the modeling paste.

SHOWING OFF
ON THE
WALL

Walls. We're surrounded by them. They protect us and keep us safe and warm. They give us a sense of security and privacy. But, sadly, they are often neglected and just stand there blank, empty, and faceless. Isn't it about time to show these steadfast guardians how much we appreciate them? They are worthy of more than just a coat of paint. And they secretly crave to be adorned and bejeweled with wonderful creations. Memory art is the perfect way to put a smile on their blank, pasty faces. We'll help you get started by sharing some beautiful pieces of art made especially for the wall. When it comes to memory art, it's time to let it all hang out! Grab a hammer and some nails and give your walls the decoration they're begging for.

This wall art is cute as a button, literally! Tania used dozens of buttons in all shapes, sizes and coordinating colors as the main embellishment for her layout. The button-covered panel offsets the focal point photo and adds a substantial feeling of texture and weight to her wall hanging. Don't be afraid to incorporate lumpy, bumpy objects on your memory art! Wall hangings like this would complement any little girl's room.

Frame

Supplies: Frame (unknown); brads, patterned paper, stickers (Karen Foster); buttons (Autumn Leaves); ink

Doll Face Tania Willis

Memory art is a great way to liven up a child's space. Greta took colors from her daughter's room and created this portrait made from a humble wooden frame, which she decorated with sweet buttons and fun accents. Unlike some adults, kids love seeing pictures of themselves, so don't forget to include memory art in their rooms. It's an easy way to personalize their domain.

Frame

Supplies: Frame (unknown); chipboard elements, patterned paper, ribbon (Fancy Pants); acrylic paint; rhinestones (Beadery); buttons (Autumn Leaves); thread

Adore Greta Hammond

Sometimes, bigger really is better! Catherine used a giant paper-mâché letter to create a unique and playful frame for this adorable wall décor for her daughter's bedroom. She continued her "big" theme by choosing big photos and bold colors for her paint and patterned paper to complement the scale of the piece. With the embellished "Elizabeth" alongside the photos, everything comes together to make a playful tribute to a darling little girl.

Paper-Mâché Letter

Supplies: Jumbo paper-mâché letter, chipboard letters (Darice); patterned paper (K&Co.); paint; butterfly, decorative tape, rhinestones, sticker (Heidi Swapp); rub-ons (Deja Views, Me & My Big Ideas); ribbons (Michaels, Offray); clip (Making Memories); adhesive foam; sandpaper

Elizabeth Catherine Feegel-Erhardt

Traditions ground us. They center us. They give us a sense of continuity and belonging. And traditions are found everywhere—even in memory art. Courtney took 12 photos of her daughter (one per month) for an entire year. She then collaged them into a piece of memory art that can be updated year after year. When next year rolls around, she says she will replace this wall hanging with the new year's batch. Voila! A tradition is born.

Cardstock and Ribbon

Just Hanging Around
Materials to use for hanging your memory art

- Ribbon
- Chain
- Wire
- Clips (like bulldog clips and paperclips)
- Grommets and string
- A wooden skirt hanger
- Rope, twine or fiber

2006 Courtney Walsh

Supplies: Cardstock; chipboard circles, patterned paper (Scenic Route); chipboard letters (Chatterbox); adhesive foam; ribbon (unknown)

Here's a sweetheart of
an idea for using a shadow
box to create memory art.
Tania painted the wooden
shadow box to complement
the layout inside. As an added feature, she adhered a
rhinestone title to the outside of the clear cover. This gives
the piece dimension and just the right touch of bling! By
using a deep frame, she was able to incorporate a hefty
wooden letter as an eye-catching accent.

Shadow Box

Supplies: Frame (Provo Craft); patterned paper (KI Memories, Li'l
Davis); embossed paper, paper frills (Doodlebug); rhinestone word (Me
& My Big Ideas); mesh (Magic Mesh); glitter glue; rub-on (Autumn
Leaves); wooden letter (unknown); paint

Sweetheart Tania Willis

Clipboards: the unsung heroes of the office supply world.
They're functional, they're reliable, they're…ugly. Hold
on a minute! Scratch that last one. Move over frames
and canvases, there's a new kid in town. Using patterned
paper, stickers, ribbons and rub-ons, Mou transformed this
unassuming clipboard from drab to fab in a few easy steps.
The best part is, you can do it too! Just grab your scraps
and some reliable adhesive and you're all set to go.

Clipboard

Supplies: Clipboard (Wal-Mart); patterned paper, rub-on letters and
numbers (Frances Meyer); rub-on accents (Luxe Designs); ribbon
(Die Cuts With A View, Offray); ink; pen

How Do I Love Thee? Mou Saha

Kids really like it when their space is personalized. It gives them a sense of pride and ownership. Vicki wanted to gift her daughter with something that would show her how special she is. This banner shows just that and totally identifies Devyn's room as her own. Vicki crafted this frilly banner using chipboard flowers and letters, patterned paper and foil accents to bling it up a bit. Hanging in a room, there'll be no question whose domain it is.

Devyn Vicki Boutin

Chipboard

Supplies: Chipboard flowers (Maya Road); chipboard letters, patterned paper (Scenic Route); buttons (Autumn Leaves); rhinestones (Westrim); foil transfer paper (Stix 2 Fantastak); ribbon (Offray); tinsel; adhesive foam

Between pigtails and playing with dolls and make-up and dating lies the "tween" years. This transitionary age can be especially challenging when creating memory art, but it's an important era to feature nonetheless. Choosing more "grown up" color palettes and sophisticated themes is a good way to accomplish this. But don't forget to add a little sweet fun and some bling. After all, growing old is mandatory…growing up is entirely optional.

Frame

Supplies: Frame (Hobby Lobby); patterned paper (Crate Paper); flower (Prima); flower center (Making Memories); word stickers (NRN); rhinestones; rub-ons (American Crafts); ink

Special Girl Christine Traversa

We live in a hustle-bustle world, so it's important to remember to slow down and take time to admire the beauty that surrounds us. Torrey's decorated tray reminds us to find joy in simple things. And by hanging on the wall, the reminder is around for all to see. To create this flowery display, Torrey die cut a variety of cardstock flowers and stamped some with a pattern. She combined these with punched greenery and lots of adhesive foam to create a dimensional floral cascade that appears to tumble out from the photo.

Take Time To Stop Torrey Scott

Wooden Tray

Supplies: Wooden tray (Creative Imaginations); cardstock; stamps (Stampendous); decorative punches; ribbon (Michaels); wooden tag (Crafts Etc.); rub-on letters (Making Memories); acrylic paint; epoxy pebbles (EK Success); adhesive foam; ink; thread

Placing this page in an album would be like putting a gallon of milk on a loaf of bread in your shopping bag. You wouldn't think about doing that, would you? Nah, and neither did Nic. Nic saved her molded ribbon technique for a layout on display to allow all the glorious ribbon dimension to pop. Molding the ribbon into curls adds a touch of whimsy to this photo-centric layout.

Just Be Beautiful You Nic Howard

Artist Canvas

Supplies: Artist canvas; cardstock; letter stickers, patterned paper (BasicGrey); chipboard letters (CherryArte, Scenic Route); ribbon, ribbon stiffener (Strano); chipboard (CherryArte); beads, brads, felt flowers (Queen & Co.); pen

Show me how! Molding Ribbon

You will need | ribbon, pencil, tape, paintbrush, fabric or ribbon stiffener

Tape one end of the ribbon to the tip of the pencil. Begin wrapping the ribbon around the pencil. As you wrap the ribbon, apply fabric stiffener to the back side of the ribbon with a brush.

When you reach the end of the pencil, tape down the free end of the ribbon. Leave the ribbon wrapped around the pencil while the fabric stiffener dries.

Once the stiffener is dry, un-tape the ends of the ribbon and slowly unwind the ribbon from the pencil. After unwinding, your ribbon will remain in a stiff curl.

Winter, spring, summer, fall…can one piece of art showcase them all? You bet! You can create simply designed displays and still showcase multiple scenes by using a series of framed art like Cindy's. Whether you hang them in a cluster or in a vertical or horizontal series, multiple frames create a cohesive collection of art that works in any room.

Celebrate Four Seasons Cindy Smith

Frames

Supplies: Frames (unknown); cardstock; patterned paper (Fontwerks, Paper Salon); stamps (Paper Salon); ink; rub-on words (Karen Foster); adhesive foam

When we think of hanging photos on a wall, what usually comes to mind are individual photos in their own separate frames. But that's not our only option. The beauty of taking scrapbooking to the wall is that we get to break photo framing boundaries. Vicki was not content to put a single photo in a frame and just leave it alone. In fact, she left the photo out of the frame entirely, and instead she decorated the glass with rub-ons. This allowed room for more than one photo, and the series of pictures really brings the story to life.

You 2 Vicki Boutin

Frame

Supplies: Frame (unknown); cardstock; patterned paper (Daisy D's, Scenic Route); stickers (Scenic Route); buttons; adhesive foam

Bright-Eyed Boy *Mou Saha*

What do you do when you really want to take that plunge from album to wall but you don't want to mess with a frame? Canvas to the rescue! Artist canvases come in all shapes and sizes and the best part is that framing isn't required. Plus, canvases are so lightweight that all you need is one small finishing nail to hang them. Take Mou's lead and choose an 8" x 8" (20cm x 20cm) pre-stretched canvas on which to adhere a simple mini layout.

Artist Canvas

Supplies: Artist canvas; letter stickers, patterned paper (Frances Meyer); chipboard letters (Heidi Swapp); ink; pen; Arial Narrow font (Microsoft)

It's hard enough to get one boy to sit still long enough for a photo, let alone three together. For kids that are always on the go, you can create the look of a group portrait without the headache by grouping individual photos together in a display like the one Kathleen put together. By using a deep shadow box, you can add as many or as few dimensional items as you wish!

Shadow Box

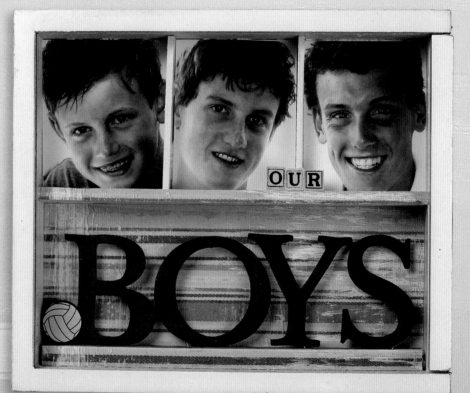

Our Boys *Kathleen Summers*

Supplies: Shadow box (Prima); patterned paper (Junkitz); chipboard letters (Scenic Route); letter stickers (Design Originals); ball brad (Hot Off The Press); ink; acrylic paint

Happy moments are the most treasured, but they can also be the most fleeting. When such a moment came for her son, Courtney knew she had to seize the opportunity and put it on display. She used lots of fabric instead of patterned paper on her wall hanging to give it a handmade feel. Ribbon tied to bulldog clips make a quick and cute hanger. Now her son can relive his happy time, anytime.

Cardstock

Be Happy Courtney Walsh

Supplies: Kraft cardstock; cardstock; patterned paper (Provo Craft); transparency (Hambly); chipboard circles (Scenic Route); clips (Making Memories); 2peas Airplane font (Two Peas in a Bucket)

Pets are an important part of the family that often get overlooked when creating memory art. We're usually so busy focusing on the people that we sometimes forget about our four-legged family members. Creating a simple, elegant tribute to furry friends can add warmth to any room in the house. Christine affixed a small layout to a pre-made wall element so it's ready to hang wherever she fancies.

The ideal
of calm exists
in a sitting cat.
-Jules Reynard

Ideal Christine Traversa

Wall Element

Supplies: Wall element (Hobby Lobby); digital patterned paper by Dani Modstad (A Cherry on Top); journaling card, stamps (Fancy Pants); ink; decorative tape (Making Memories); rhinestones; circle punch; Century Gothic font (Microsoft); image editing software (Adobe)

Illuminated letters graced the printed page for centuries, but then they became a lost art form. Thanks to scrapbooking and memory art, they are enjoying a renaissance of sorts. We now have tons of chipboard alphas to dress and thousands of fonts available to use. Even better are the oversized monogram letters that have hit the market. With these as a foundation, Mou grabbed some pretty papers, stickers, rub-ons and other scrapbooking staples and made this ARTistic display.

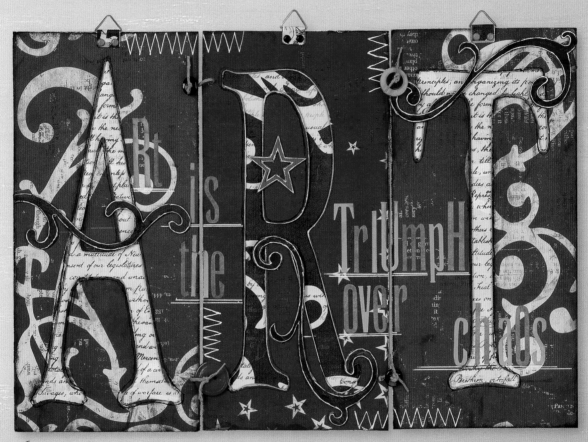

Art Mou Saha

Chipboard Monograms

Supplies: Buttons, chipboard, letter stickers, monogram letters, patterned paper (Rusty Pickle); acrylic paint; brads; mini hangers (Jo-Ann); hemp cord (Darice); acrylic paint; decoupage medium; ink; pen

As designers, we are sometimes accused of using everything but the kitchen sink. Barb comes close to that accusation! To make her art, she went into the kitchen and grabbed a cookie sheet. She combined stickers, buttons and embellishments to transform this unassuming kitchen utensil into a fun, yet useful perpetual calendar. The great thing is, by fitting elements with magnetic backings, you can change the calendar's design whenever you want.

One Month Barb Hogan

Cookie Sheet

Supplies: Cookie sheet; cardstock; chipboard accents (Imagination Project); number stickers (American Crafts, Arctic Frog, Creative Imaginations, Creative Memories, Imagination Project, Pebbles, Sticker Studio, Wordsworth); buttons (Hobby Lobby, Making Memories); ribbon (American Crafts, Making Memories, May Arts, Michaels); ink; magnets (Staples)

We all have stuff plastered to the fronts of our refrigerators—coupons, photos, kids' artwork and tons of magnets. Isn't it about time to elevate this display area to be a thing of beauty, instead of an unorganized eyesore? Kathleen sure thought so when she created this magnetized layout for the fridge. The kitchen is more than just a cooking station; it's a gathering place and the heart of many family homes. When it comes to memory art for a room, try displaying memories of the room itself.

Chipboard

Supplies: Cardstock; patterned paper (Die Cuts With A View); letter and arrow stamps (Inque Boutique); ink; magnetic snaps (BasicGrey)

The Kitchen Kathleen Summers

It's time to look around and see things in terms of their form and not their intended function. Samantha took this concept to heart when she roped, tied and branded this tray for a new purpose—a frame for her memory art. She carefully chose the papers and colors to match her daughter's room, then adhered them to a painted wooden tray to create this rootin'-tootin' wall hanging that's sure to please even the most discriminating little cowgirl.

Cowgirl Samantha Walker

Wooden Tray

Supplies: Serving tray, chipboard letters, patterned paper (Creative Imaginations); cardstock; paints; ink; adhesive foam

Out of Bounds
Unusual items to frame your art

- Cookie sheet
- Muffin tin
- Dinner, dessert or charger plate
- Old window

- Mirror
- Hardware store finds
- Rulers
- Serving tray

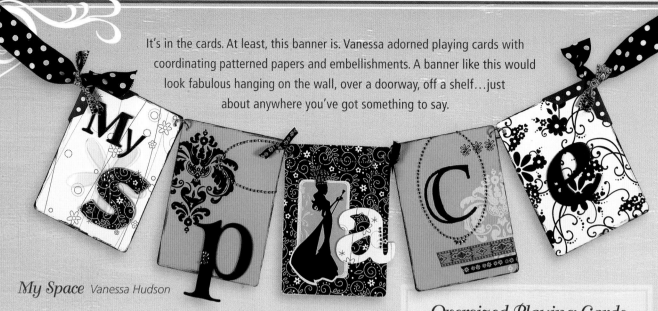

It's in the cards. At least, this banner is. Vanessa adorned playing cards with coordinating patterned papers and embellishments. A banner like this would look fabulous hanging on the wall, over a doorway, off a shelf…just about anywhere you've got something to say.

My Space Vanessa Hudson

Oversized Playing Cards

Supplies: Cardstock; patterned paper (Doodlebug); flower, photo corners, playing cards, rhinestones, stickers (Heidi Swapp); chipboard letters (BasicGrey, Cosmo Cricket, Heidi Swapp); ribbon (BasicGrey, Offray); jump rings; paint

There are probably things hidden in your kitchen that you never use. So dive into the cupboards' depths to find treasures to repurpose for display. Alecia took a charger plate (you know, those big, decorative plates that sit under real plates and look fancy) and transformed it into a fabulous dimensional frame to house a mini layout. She finished the project by adhering coordinating ribbon to the back of the plate to act as a hanger.

Charger Plate

Supplies: Charger plate (Target); mesh (Magic Mesh); acrylic frame, patterned paper (KI Memories); chipboard letters (Me & My Big Ideas); ribbon (unknown); sequins (Darice); label maker (Around The Block); glitter; buttons (Autumn Leaves, vintage); beads; flower (Heidi Swapp)

Spunky Girl Alecia Ackerman Grimm

What's so different about this layout for the wall? Well, it's the wall! You can see the wall right through the project since the layout is transparent. Vanessa used a printed transparency as the base for her memory art to allow the beauty of the room to literally shine through. She suspended the layout from hooks in a deep frame. This kind of art looks fabulous in any room because it always blends with the décor.

Frame and Transparency

Be True to You Vanessa Hudson

Supplies: Frame (Hobby Lobby); transparency (Hambly); cardstock; chipboard letters, large dot accents (Heidi Swapp); patterned circles (Doodlebug); brads, flowers (Queen & Co.); clothing tags; screw-in hooks (hardware store); pen

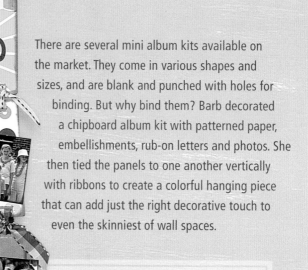

There are several mini album kits available on the market. They come in various shapes and sizes, and are blank and punched with holes for binding. But why bind them? Barb decorated a chipboard album kit with patterned paper, embellishments, rub-on letters and photos. She then tied the panels to one another vertically with ribbons to create a colorful hanging piece that can add just the right decorative touch to even the skinniest of wall spaces.

Chipboard Mini Album

Supplies: Chipboard album (Kaiser); patterned paper (KI Memories); flowers (Prima); ribbon (American Crafts, May Arts, Michaels); ink; rub-ons (Imagination Project); brads; pen

Field Day Barb Hogan

Memory art comes in all shapes and sizes. It doesn't need to be big to get noticed. This cute decorated hanging tin really draws the viewer in with its peekaboo photo feature. Tiffany poked two holes in the tin's top and secured the frame to the tin top with brads. You can either leave the tin closed for a fun frame, or you can insert a mini book inside to house extra photos—a treasure just waiting to be discovered.

Supplies: Tin (KI Memories); brads, frame (BasicGrey); big brad (Hot Off The Press); chipboard shape (Li'l Davis); ribbon (unknown)

Metal Tin

Portrait Tiffany Tillman

Clipboard

Clipboards have really come into their own as a platform on which to build memory art. They have found their niche right between decorated frames and shadow boxes as a means for display. By extending the decorations of her photo montage onto the clip, the clipboard itself becomes part of the art, not just a support for it. This clipboard creation is the perfect medium to herald the transition from childhood to teen years—not too juvenile and not too grown-up.

(in be) Tween Barb Hogan

Supplies: Clipboard (Melissa Frances); patterned paper (American Crafts, Autumn Leaves, Crate Paper, K&Co., Me & My Big Ideas); chipboard letters (Collage Press); rub-ons (Imagination Project); brads (K&Co.); flowers (Michaels, Prima); ribbon (American Crafts); foam spacer; image editing software (Adobe)

Free Spirit Nic Howard

What can we do when we have a treasured photo that's just too special to close up in an album? We can enlarge it, frame it and hang it on the wall. Or we can enlarge it, create a gorgeous layout around it and then hang it on the wall. Nic took a favorite photo and turned it into a showpiece for her home. The supporting layout not only brings the photo meaning, but sets it off beautifully for all to see and enjoy.

Artist Canvas

Supplies: Canvas; cardstock; patterned paper (BasicGrey, Scenic Route); letter stickers (Adornit); rub-ons (BasicGrey, Fancy Pants, My Mind's Eye, Rhonna Farrer); rickrack (Fancy Pants); brads, flowers (Queen & Co.); ink; pen

One thing modern designers stress is simplicity of design. If a design is strong, it stands on its own without adding bells, whistles, lights and sirens. The same goes for memory art. Finding ourselves free from the confines of the album, we may be tempted to include lots of stuff on our art just because we can. But this doesn't ensure that the finished product will be appealing. Sometimes less is more. In those cases, remember to K.I.S.S. Keep it simple, sister.

Artist Canvas

Supplies: Canvas; cardstock; patterned paper (BasicGrey, unknown); rub-ons (Autumn Leaves); rickrack; button, chipboard letters (unknown); book page

Love Sarah van Wijck

Organization is always challenging, especially when it comes to keeping your kids organized. Catherine came up with a fun idea to keep her daughters' clutter ordered! She personalized a hanging rack to entice those little hands to hang up their accessories. Catherine turned an unpainted wooden rack into a rustically beautiful, yet functional workhorse by using acrylic paint and sandpaper to distress the piece. Then she created mini layouts with the girls' pictures to turn the rack into memory art.

Wooden Rack

Erhardt Girls *Catherine Feegel-Erhardt*

Supplies: Frame (unknown); patterned paper (Martha Stewart); transparencies (Hambly); ribbons (BasicGrey, Making Memories); decorative tape (Heidi Swapp); buttons, tag (unknown); thread; paint

Frames are a staple when it comes to memory art, but they can get pricey, especially when you choose a large size. Thrift stores, garage sales and flea markets are perfect places to find inexpensive frames of all sizes. Don't worry if they are a little beat up or not quite the right color. Gretchen sanded her thrifty find then painted it black. She removed the backing but left the glass in place and affixed stickers, photos and rub-on elements directly to the glass to create a great peekaboo wall accent.

Thrift Store Frame

Beautiful Borders
Choosing and using frames

- When in doubt, take a hint from art galleries; use basic black gallery frames.

- To emphasize a creation, place it in an oversized frame and use a wide, white mat.

- Take an ornate or antique frame and use ribbon to suspend a layout inside.

- If you don't want the frame to show, try clear acrylic frames or glass frames.

- Love the frame but it's too flat to house your dimensional piece? Just leave the glass out altogether.

- Try non-glare glass. It's available in most framing and craft stores.

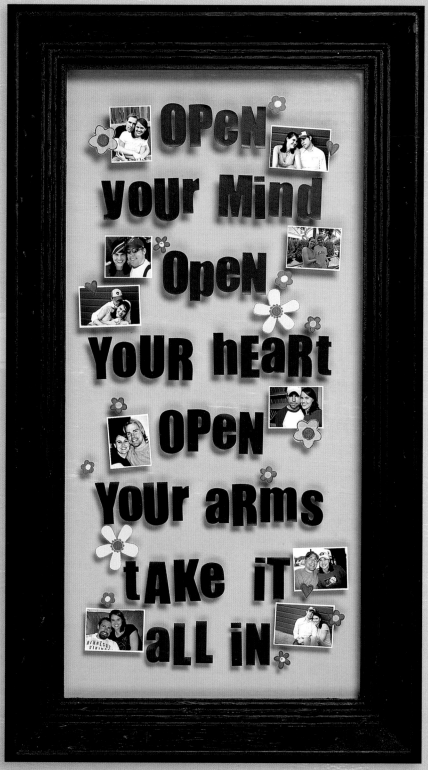

Take It All In Gretchen McElveen

Supplies: Frame (unknown); letter stickers (Scenic Route); rub-ons (Junkitz)

The great thing about a blank canvas is that it's just that—a blank canvas. Artist canvases are such a great foundation for memory art. They're readily available, inexpensive and can accommodate just about any medium you throw at them. Gretchen used basic scrapbooking supplies including patterned paper, cardstock, stamps, stickers and paint to create this joyous reminder that life is not to be taken for granted. Hanging on her wall, it will remind her of this important sentiment every time she looks at it.

Artist Canvas

Supplies: Canvas; scalloped cardstock (Bazzill, Die Cuts With A View); patterned paper (BasicGrey, Chatterbox, Creative Imaginations, Junkitz, Two Peas in a Bucket); letter stamps (Fontwerks); letter stickers (hardware store); acrylic paint; ink

Live It Gretchen McElveen

When life hands you lemons…make memory art! When you have a picture of someone you love but the background is not appealing, you can still turn it into art. Suzy loved this photo of her daughter but hated the background. So she cut out a portion of the photo and mounted it onto a canvas that she had decorated with paint, chipboard flowers, ribbon and buttons. For a fun finish, she dotted a sweet, simple border for the canvas using white paint.

Artist Canvas

Supplies: Canvas; acrylic paints; chipboard flowers (Maya Road); buttons (Autumn Leaves); rickrack; plaid ribbon (Li'l Davis); adhesive foam; pen

Chloe Suzy Plantamura

There are so many round things associated with summer—the sun, beach balls, sand dollars, inner tubes, sea shells—that Samantha decided that a square format for her summer memory plaque just wouldn't do. Taking cues from things around us is a great tip when deciding what shape to use for our memory art projects. Organic shapes have a softer feel and lend visual interest to our creations.

Summer Hawaii 2007 Samantha Walker

Wooden Plaque

Supplies: Ribbon plaques, chipboard letters, journaling sticker, paper clips, patterned paper, sticker tabs (Creative Imaginations); ribbon (Offray); circle punches; ink; pen

Love the Beach Christine Traversa

What happens when you take a favorite memory, a touching quote and an eye-catching design and roll them all together? You get memory art that is perfect for displaying outside your album. Christine combined a design cut from patterned paper with stamps to create a small, but dramatic piece of art to hang on her wall. It's a piece she hopes her daughters will look at over the years and remember the good times.

Wooden Square

Supplies: Square wall element (Hobby Lobby); patterned paper (EK Success); button (unknown); stamps (Fancy Pants); ink; pen; Afternoon Delight font (Autumn Leaves)

A frame is sometimes a boring necessity for displaying art on the wall. But they don't have to be lackluster. Many scrapbook supply companies now make blank frames that are specifically designed to be decorated. By decorating this frame, Vicki created the look of a scrapbook layout around the framed photo, complete with texture. The clear buttons and rolled paper edges give just the right dimensional touch to this hot summertime creation.

Beach Babe *Vicki Boutin*

Canvas Frame

Supplies: Frame (Creative Imaginations); cardstock; chipboard, patterned paper (Scenic Route); buttons (Autumn Leaves); acrylic paint

Remember when homemade decorations for the holidays consisted of construction paper chains and paper angel banners? Paper decorations are not a new concept, but using your scrapbook supplies to create holiday decorations breathes new life into the classic genre of holiday paper crafting. The options are endless, too. From banners to hang in windows (like this one Cari made), to wreaths, luminaria and ornaments for the tree, paper crafting is a joyous way for the whole family to make holidays more festive.

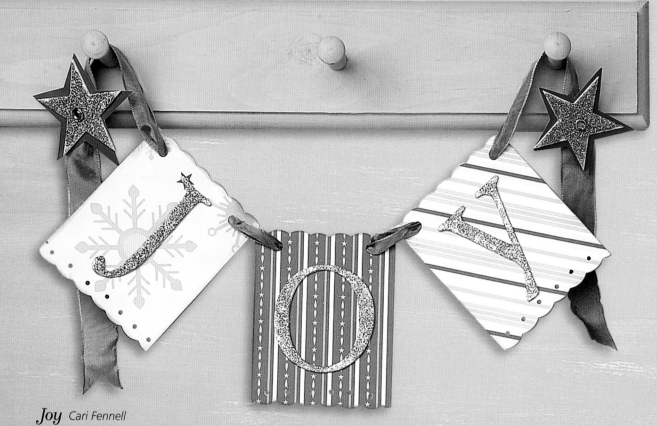

Joy *Cari Fennell*

Cardstock

Supplies: Cardstock; patterned paper (Paper Salon); chipboard letters (Rusty Pickle); chipboard stars (Accu-Cut); rhinestone brads (Making Memories); glitter; decorative scissors; ribbon (Offray)

Are you one of those people who decorates her house for every seasonal occasion? No? Well, why not? Seasonal layouts like Cari's are a wonderfully simple way to decorate your home for any holiday. Just take your seasonal layouts and hang them on the wall! When the seasons change, so can the displayed layouts. Cari created this fun layout by using masks on metallic paper and spray painting over them. When she lifted the masks away, they revealed sparkly snowflakes that are the perfect accent for this playful winter page.

A Snowy Day Cari Fennell

Metallic Paper

Supplies: Cardstock; brackets, metallic paper (Trace Industries); chipboard and rub-on letters, decorative tape, snowflake accents (Heidi Swapp); spray paint; rhinestones; buttons (Autumn Leaves); chipboard star (Accu Cut); glitter; acrylic paint

Welcome to the new millennium of memory art where artists turn the shelves themselves into beautiful things! Jodi converted a display shelf into a work of art by adding paint, metallic rub-ons and antique chipboard elements to its face. By nestling a layout in the back of the frame, Jodi brought significance and honor to the objects displayed on the shelf.

Arnold Jodi Amidei

Display Shelf

Supplies: Frame (unknown); cardstock; patterned paper (Hot Off The Press); ribbon (EK Success); metal nail heads (K&Co.); chipboard letters (Heidi Swapp); chipboard shapes (Paper Studio); acrylic paint; crackle finish; rub-ons (Craf-T); glasses (Crafts Etc.); pocket watch (unknown)

$\mathcal{S}$how me how! Antiquing Chipboard

You will need | acrylic paint (black and gold), chipboard piece, brush, crackle medium

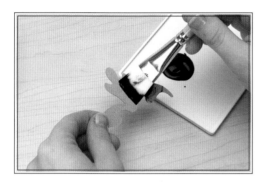

Brush a thick layer of black acrylic paint over the chipboard piece. Add a second coat of paint as needed to completely cover the chipboard. Let the paint dry before applying the crackle medium.

Brush the crackle medium over the painted chipboard. For a subtle crackle, apply a thin coat of medium. For a bolder look, apply more medium.

When the crackle medium becomes tacky, brush gold paint over the chipboard and allow it to dry.

Collage frames are so convenient—the overall layout is already decided for you. Now that the hard part is done, you can concentrate on creating art. Greta carefully chose colors and embellishments that would complement her photos and layered the elements to create visual interest. Imagine how boring this piece would have been had photos simply been placed in the frame openings. The beauty of ready-made products is that they act as blank canvases for you to artfully transform.

Memories Greta Hammond

Collage Frame

Supplies: Frame (unknown); patterned paper (Crate Paper, EK Success); rub-on words (Daisy D's, Scenic Route); chipboard pieces (EK Success, Li'l Davis); brads (K&Co.); felt stickers (EK Success); digital frames by Rhonna Farrer (Two Peas in a Bucket)

Collage frames are cool, but what if you can't find the right one? Create the same look with frames that you arrange and hang together yourself! Nic removed the glass from her frames to give her dimensional mini-creations some breathing room. To ensure good overall design, she arranged them on a tabletop and worked on them simultaneously. She tied the frames together with ribbon and hung them off a mesh rod for display.

Aden Nic Howard

Frames

Supplies: Frames (unknown); mesh rod (hardware store); cardstock; patterned paper (We R Memory Keepers); letter stickers (Adornit); rub-ons (Creative Imaginations, Fancy Pants, Scenic Route); ribbon (Heidi Swapp, unknown)

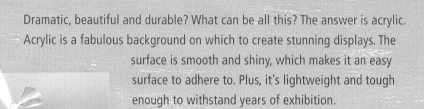

Dramatic, beautiful and durable? What can be all this? The answer is acrylic. Acrylic is a fabulous background on which to create stunning displays. The surface is smooth and shiny, which makes it an easy surface to adhere to. Plus, it's lightweight and tough enough to withstand years of exhibition.

Acrylic Sheet

Supplies: Perspex sheet (unknown); patterned paper (Daisy D's); rub-ons (BasicGrey); chipboard (Maya Road); rhinestones (Heidi Swapp); tag (Making Memories); button, beads, ribbon (unknown)

Dreaming Sarah van Wijck

Sophie Suzy Plantamura

Displays don't have to be complex. Sometimes beauty lies in simplicity. Suzy wanted to enhance this photo without overpowering it. Her solution was to frame a simple, dimensional layout using the photo as the centerpiece. To display the art, she removed the glass from the frame to prevent elements from getting flat.

Frame

Supplies: Frame (Wilton Industries); flowers, patterned paper (Martha Stewart); ribbon (Heidi Swapp, unknown); thread

What can you do when you want the look of dimension but don't have the luxury of using a shadow box or other dimensional platform? Digital elements to the rescue! Take a tip from Tiffany. There are so many great-looking digital scrapbooking supplies available for download that it's easier than ever to create the look of layers in only two dimensions. All you need is software, photo paper, and a printer to create realistic looking effects.

Lita Tiffany Tillman

Matted Frame

Supplies: Frame (Target); digital paper (artist's own design);
digital paper tears by Jen Caputo (Scrapbook Graphics)

Memory art is great for decorating our homes, but it's even better when we give it away as gifts. The next time you're stumped for a personal, heart-felt gift to give a loved one, how about making them a piece of memory art to display? Courtney made this lovely shadow box collection of her family as a Christmas gift. Memory art is so much better than handing someone a single photo in a plain frame!

Our Family Courtney Walsh

Shadow Box

Supplies: Frame (unknown); patterned paper (Chatterbox); letter stickers (American Crafts, Doodlebug); ribbon (Offray); flowers (Prima); snap (KI Memories); key (Rusty Pickle); ink; pins

Baroque-style antique frames are stunning by themselves. Couple them with a striking layout and you've created a dramatic piece of art for a room. Amy found this vintage frame at an antique fair and knew right away that she wanted to use it to showcase her memory art. She created her layout and mounted it on chipboard for stability, then tied on the title for a little added flair. To complete the piece, Amy suspended the layout from the frame using velvet ribbon.

Family Amy Peterman

Vintage Frame

Supplies: Frame (vintage); matte board; chipboard letters, lace, patterned paper, ribbon, rub-ons, stamps (Fancy Pants); acrylic paint; floss; ink; adhesive foam

When it comes to memory art, it's so easy to create the perfect look to go with any decorating style. Tiffany chose a monochromatic color scheme for her wall layout to match the décor of the room it will hang in. By turning the photos black and white, Tiffany ensured that they would match any color scheme. A simple, uncluttered title is all the embellishment this compilation needs to make it picture-perfect.

Acrylic Frame

Supplies: Frame (Pageframe); cardstock; patterned paper, rub-ons (Urban Lily); chipboard letters (Queen & Co.); ribbon (Michaels); ink

I Love My Family Tiffany Tillman

We're so used to creating in a square format that we don't realize we've set up boundaries. The beauty of memory art is that we can step outside the box and create in any size! Tania used an elongated frame, which houses her wallet-sized photos just perfectly.

Love Tania Willis

Frame

Supplies: Frame (Wal-Mart); embossed paper (Doodlebug); rub-on word (Li'l Davis); rub-on accents (KI Memories); button brad (Karen Foster); floss

Wreaths aren't just for Christmas anymore. Kathleen created her timeless picture wreath using favorite photos, a few stickers, a stamped design and a Styrofoam base. It's easy to re-create this versatile piece of décor. And don't worry if the colors in the photos don't coordinate. Simply convert the photos to black and white using photo editing software. This not only gives the whole piece a sense of unity, but it also lends an air of timelessness that will withstand any decorating trend.

The Summers Family Kathleen Summers

Cardstock and Styrofoam

Supplies: Cardstock; letter stickers (BasicGrey); flourish stamp (Inque Boutique); ink; Styrofoam board

Even the smallest framed photos can make a statement. Shadow boxes are a dramatic way to showcase a treasured photo. When Sandi realized that she didn't have a current photo of herself and her husband, she remedied the disgrace by setting up her tripod and snapping some photos of them together. Then, using a few simple scrapbooking supplies, she transformed her favorite photo into a glowing tribute by using a small shadow box to showcase the new work of art.

Shadow Box

Supplies: Shadow box (Hallmark); cardstock; chipboard word, patterned paper (Die Cuts With A View); chipboard heart, rhinestones (Heidi Swapp); cardboard; clip

Love Sandi Minchuk

What time is it? It's time to create a functional piece of memory art that's as beautiful as it is timeless. Samantha embellished a square-faced clock with coordinating patterned papers, chipboard elements, rickrack and epoxy stickers. She added small black-and-white photos at key points on the clock face to enhance both its interest and function. Family time is precious time, so why not preserve every second of it!

Unfinished Wood Clock

Supplies: Clock, cardstock, chipboard letters, epoxy stickers, patterned paper, ribbon (Creative Imaginations); Kraft cardstock; adhesive foam; rickrack

Family Time Samantha Walker

Ready-made frames usually come with a mat and a chipboard backing. Most people are content to just slide a photo under the mat, secure the backing in place and call it a day. Not scrapbookers! Alecia covered her frame's chipboard backing with diagonal strips of coordinating patterned paper, then cut the ivory mat down to let the decorated backing act as a second mat for her project. Not finished there, she embellished her mat and added a title to create a truly one-of-a-kind piece of art.

Grandparents Alecia Ackerman Grimm

Matted Frame

Supplies: Frame (Michaels); patterned paper (Adornit); word stickers (7gypsies); stamps (Heidi Swapp, Li'l Davis); acrylic word (Heidi Swapp); rub-on stitching (Die Cuts With A View); photo corners; ink

Shadow boxes are a great way to house and display dimensional works of art. Their depth allows for layer upon layer of texture. Amy took full advantage of this feature in her shadow box creation by using foam adhesive to lift each layer of her memory art from the underlying one. This adds an incredible amount of depth and interest to her piece. To finish it off, she chose to pin her layout in place with map pins, giving her art the look of a museum-quality display.

Shadow Box

Me and My Shadow (Box)
Things to consider when using a shadow box

- Make your own with decorative molding, chipboard, a staple gun and glue.

- Turn any box on end for an instant shadow box.

- Look around your house for materials to make unusual shadow boxes. Cookie cutters make darling shaped mini shadow boxes. Also try baskets, rulers glued together, planters or jars.

- Don't forget that round, oval, triangular, hexagonal or other polygon shapes make great shadow boxes.

- Be on the lookout for flea market treasures. Many objects can be "gutted" to create interesting shadow boxes like radios, book covers, tins, tackle boxes and dresser drawers.

Love Amy Peterman

Supplies: Shadow box (Pottery Barn); cardstock; brads, buttons, chipboard letters and accents, crocheted flower, patterned paper, pins, ribbon, stamps (Fancy Pants); paint; transparency; adhesive foam; ink; pen

Memory art can be a timeless and precious gift for someone you love. Genevieve created this sophisticated framed piece as a gift for her mom. She used bits and pieces from her scrapbooking supply cache. And it didn't take much, either—a sticker here, a scrap of patterned paper there, throw in an embellishment or two and she had the makings of a beautiful collage. Subtle shades and textures lend an air of elegance and tranquility to this lovely gift that her mom is sure to treasure for years to come.

Experiment #59 *Genevieve Simmonds*

Frame

Supplies: Frame (unknown); handmade paper; corrugated cardboard; patterned paper (7gypsies, Daisy D's); sticker, tag (7gypsies); chipboard heart, decorative tape (Heidi Swapp); masking tape; stamps (Purple Onion); paint, foil, fibers, lace; gesso

Moments throughout our lives are fleeting. So what better way to capture a precious moment than to turn it into a clock? It's a fun way to give something that is functional a much-needed face lift. Don't let time slip away! Jodi grabbed her leftover supplies and turned a plain clock into a showpiece. She used alcohol inks to give the triangular foil accents a unique look.

Clock Parts

Supplies: Clock (unknown); cardstock; metal foil (Amaco); letter and number stamps (Paper Studio); stamps (Autumn Leaves); inks; adhesive foam

Time's Up!
Using clocks in memory art

- Decorate clock faces however you want to suit your style, theme or color scheme.

- Use large chipboard or stamped numbers, or you can choose to use no numbers at all.

- Change the look of hands by overlaying them with cut-out paper shapes.

- Turn just about any object into a clock! Kits that include a motor, hands and face are available at craft stores.

- Feeling really brave? Try altering a pocket watch or wrist watch.

Time *Jodi Amidei*

Show me how! Making an Alcohol Ink Design

You will need | alcohol ink in at least two colors, alcohol ink applicator, three alcohol ink applicator felts, metal foil

Begin by adding a few drops of your first color of ink to the felt applicator.

Tap the applicator in small motions on the metal foil. Apply the ink in a random pattern.

Replace the felt tip on the applicator and add a few drops of your second color. Tap that color on the metal foil in a random pattern. Repeat this step to add additional colors.

Chipboard

Scrapbookers are a resourceful lot. We are always looking for ways to recycle, reuse, repurpose or renew objects. Suzy loved this picture of her daughter, and even though she had already scrapped it, she wanted to turn it into a piece of art she could hang in her office. Being the resourceful scrapbooker that she is, she used the leftover negative of a chipboard tag set to create the frame. Its small openings allowed Suzy to add additional photos. How clever!

Chloe Suzy Plantamura

Supplies: Chipboard frame (Fancy Pants); patterned paper (Sassafras Lass); flowers (Bazzill); chipboard page (Maya Road); chipboard flowers and photo corners (Making Memories); buttons (Buttons Galore); ribbon, rickrack (unknown); floss; ink

When looking in a craft store for frames, your first stop can be the clearance bin. Afterall, you're going to change the frame anyway, right? Sandi came across these frames in the clearance section of a major craft store. Their surface size allowed for tons of embellishments around the photo openings. Sandi used a variety of patterned papers, embellishments, fabric trim, buttons and painted wooden letters to create this matching set of altered frames.

Frames

Supplies: Frames; cardstock; cardstock flowers, patterned paper, scalloped cardstock (Die Cuts With A View); wooden letters (Provo Craft); chipboard tag (Sweetwater); brads, plastic flowers (Queen & Co.); paper flowers (Prima); buttons (My Mind's Eye); piping (Wrights); ribbon, rickrack (May Arts); chipboard swirls (Fancy Pants); fabric flower (Bazzill); rub-on word (Scenic Route); charms (unknown); rhinestones (Heidi Swapp)

Madison and Sadie Sandi Minchuk

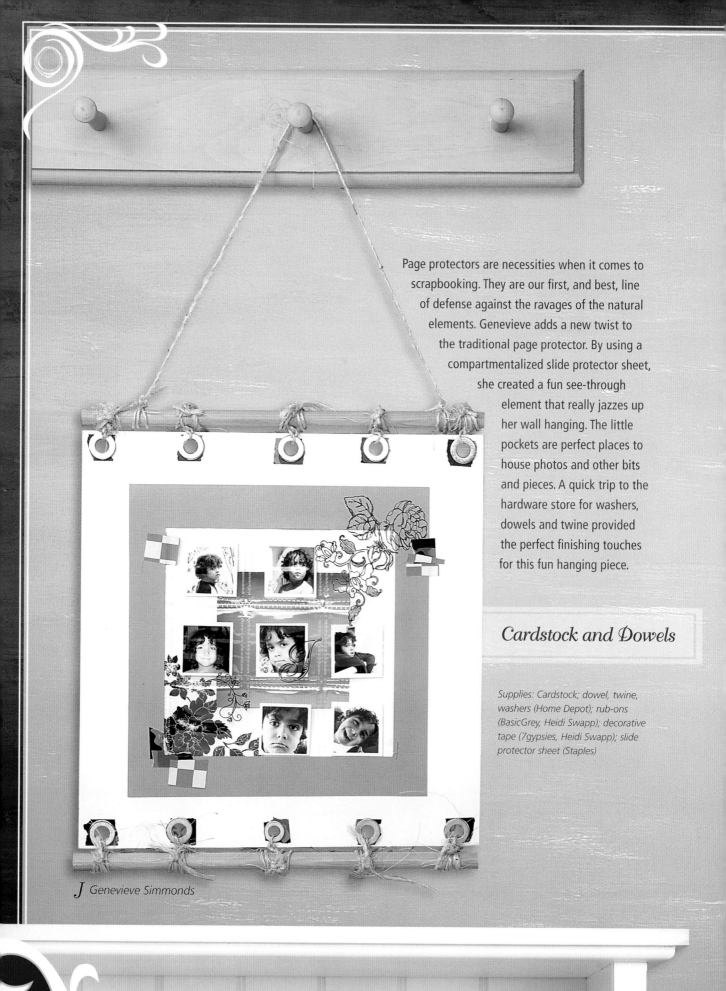

Page protectors are necessities when it comes to scrapbooking. They are our first, and best, line of defense against the ravages of the natural elements. Genevieve adds a new twist to the traditional page protector. By using a compartmentalized slide protector sheet, she created a fun see-through element that really jazzes up her wall hanging. The little pockets are perfect places to house photos and other bits and pieces. A quick trip to the hardware store for washers, dowels and twine provided the perfect finishing touches for this fun hanging piece.

Cardstock and Dowels

Supplies: Cardstock; dowel, twine, washers (Home Depot); rub-ons (BasicGrey, Heidi Swapp); decorative tape (7gypsies, Heidi Swapp); slide protector sheet (Staples)

J Genevieve Simmonds

Making layouts to hang on the wall affords us options—options for size, shape, depth and even weight. Vanessa took advantage of her freedom and used transparent "paper" as part of her layout. She sewed felt flowers onto the transparent part of the page to give the illusion that they were floating on air. She also used a wooden pant hanger as a uniquely perfect way to hang the layout.

Beauty

that comes from Within

july 2007

Beauty Vanessa Hudson

Hanger and Transparency

Supplies: Cardstock; patterned paper (Autumn Leaves, K&Co.); transparency (Hambly); chipboard letters (Heidi Swapp); felt flowers (American Crafts); brads, paper clip, ribbon (K&Co.); hanger; pen

SHOWING OFF around the HOUSE

Interior design is no longer limited to window treatments, upholstery, wallpaper and paint. It's time to include memory art in the mix. With scrapbooking supplies, it's easy for us to create memory art for anywhere and everywhere. The vast array of choices ensures that our projects will meld perfectly with any décor. Take a good look around and search out all those nooks and crannies that are in need of a decorator's hand and a personal touch. We all have those special photos that just beg to be showcased. Sure, we could stick them in a ready-made frame and sit them on a shelf. But that's not us. We are scrapbookers. We just don't know how to leave things alone. And why should we, anyway? It's time to leave our creative mark all over the house.

"Mom, look what I can do!" How many times do you hear this phrase a day? Kids are so proud of their accomplishments. Isn't it about time to show a special child how proud we are of them? It's not hard, and it can have a profound effect on budding little self-esteems. All it takes are a few action photos, some hard-earned memorabilia and a shadow box to create a glowing tribute to someone you love.

Shadow Box

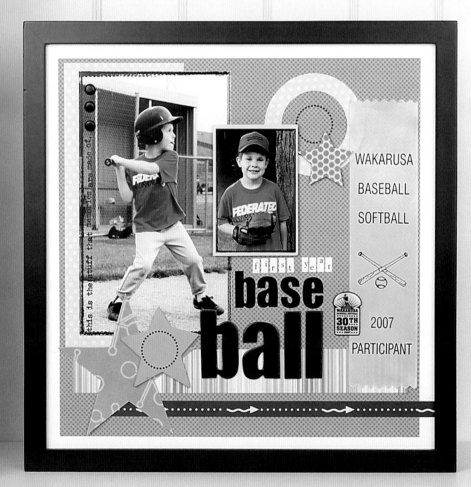

Supplies: Shadow box (unknown); cardstock; chipboard letters, patterned paper (Scenic Route); chipboard stars (Maya Road); letter stickers (Making Memories, Scenic Route); rub-ons (American Crafts, Creative Imaginations); acrylic paint; brads; digital frames by Rhonna Farrer (Two Peas in a Bucket)

Baseball Greta Hammond

Martial arts, like many physical activities, teaches its students about more than just physical conditioning—it can hold valuable life lessons as well. Barb understood this and took advantage of the opportunity by creating this thoughtful tribute to a taekwondo adventure. She used a coasterboard album as the base. Coasterboard is chipboard's cousin, but it's smoother, more uniform, and denser than chipboard, so it accepts inks and paints beautifully. Give it a try!

Supplies: Mini album, chipboard shapes, rub-ons (Imagination Project); ribbon (Michaels); pen

Since most of us scrapbookers are women, we tend toward layouts with a feminine flair. This approach doesn't quite work when the subject matter is 100% male. On these occassions we just have to leave off the flowers and hearts and opt for more masculine features. But masculine doesn't mean a piece has to be plain. Using bold, rich colors and embellishments in metal is a sure-fire way to decorate a masculine project and still have it turn out beautiful.

Frame

TKD Chix *Barb Hogan*

Alex *Barb Hogan*

Supplies: Frame (unknown); patterned paper, photo turns (7gypsies); epoxy letter stickers (Creative Imaginations); ribbon (Stampin' Up); tag (EK Success); beads; metal accents (Making Memories, Maya Road); paint

Chipboard Accordion Album

Welcome to the fold! With lots of pages, this simple accordion-fold album is perfect to showcase a holiday or special event like a child's birthday. Alecia made certain none of the elements on the pages stuck out of the bottom so that the album can sit squarely on a tabletop or mantle. She even enlarged all the text so that people can view the pages from a distance without having to pick up the album. Let the party begin!

Supplies: Book (Rusty Pickle); cardstock; page tabs, patterned paper (Die Cuts With A View); letter stickers (Doodlebug, Me & My Big Ideas); mesh (Magic Mesh); label maker (Around The Block); 3D stickers (Me & My Big Ideas); rub-ons (Junkitz); ribbon (SEI); star punch

Birthday Bash Alecia Ackerman Grimm

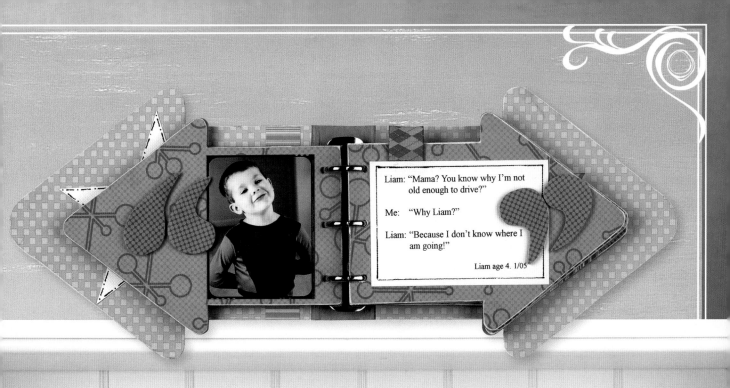

Liam: "Mama? You know why I'm not old enough to drive?"

Me: "Why Liam?"

Liam: "Because I don't know where I am going!"

Liam age 4. 1/05

Even though it's hip to be square, why not try another shape for your display albums? While square formats are easy to work with, they can be a little boring. Greta found this funky arrow-shaped chipboard album and knew she wanted to fill it with something as equally intriguing. Sitting on a coffee table, this album just begs to be opened and explored…and once inside, the reader will giggle along with the silly quotes.

Chipboard Mini Album

Supplies: Album, ribbon (Maya Road); patterned paper, rub-ons (Scenic Route); letter stickers (Making Memories); chipboard letters and shapes (Maya Road, Scenic Route); buttons (Autumn Leaves); brad (Queen & Co.); fabric tabs (Scrapworks); digital frames by Rhonna Farrer (Two Peas in a Bucket); Times New Roman font (Microsoft)

Have enough mini albums adorning your home? Give this format a try! Alecia's photo cube is like a mini album complete with six small layouts. But for a fun twist, she placed each of the tiny layouts on the face of a cube. This is one square mini album that thinks outside of the box.

Cardboard Cube

Supplies: Photo cube (Making Memories); patterned paper (Adornit, Autumn Leaves, KI Memories); stickers (K&Co., KI Memories, Scenic Route); thought bubble stickers (Bam Pop)

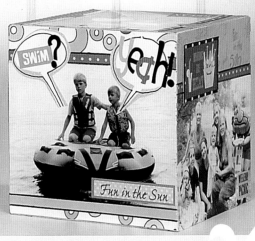

What Did You Say? Greta Hammond

Summertime Alecia Ackerman Grimm

Making a mini album doesn't require pre-made albums and tons of embellishments. Take a tip from Sarah. She created this simple yet striking mini album using a few basic supplies like watercolor paper, ribbon and a bit of patterned paper. By transforming her photos to black and white, and keeping them large on the page, she turned the focus on the photos and made her simple album very striking indeed.

Supplies: Watercolor paper; patterned paper (Jenni Bowlin); ribbon (unknown); stamp (7gypsies); digital stamps (artist's own design)

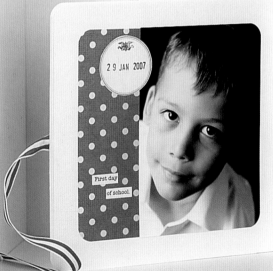

One Year Sarah van Wijck

Show me how!

Making an Easy Cardstock Mini Album

You will need

2 sheets of cardstock, paper trimmer, corner rounder, bone folder, sewing machine, thread, scissors, adhesive, ribbon

Note: The steps below show how to create a 6" x 6" (15cm x 15cm) album. To make a larger album, like the one shown at the left, you will need paper wider than 6" (15cm), such as watercolor paper.

Cut two sheets of 12" x 12" (30cm x 30cm) cardstock (plain or patterned) in half. Round the corners. Then fold the four pieces in half to create square pages. Use a bone folder to set the crease.

Unfold the four sheets and stack them. Using a sewing machine, sew a straight stitch down the center of the stack.

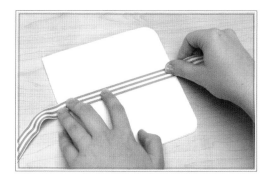

Cut a length of ribbon to about 32" (81cm). Attach the ribbon along the center of the front and back covers of the album leaving tails on the right side of the album for tying.

This castle-shaped album is a perfect example of how, with a few artistic touches, an album really can be any theme you want it to be. On page 118, Samantha Walker made this mini album look like a sand castle, but here, Tania turned it into a fairy princess castle simply by choosing bright feminine colors and embellishments. Shaped albums are so versatile and can be adapted to any theme, color scheme, mood or style. All it takes is adding your own creative touch.

Supplies: Album (Creative Imaginations); textured paper (Fibermark); brads, patterned paper, rub-ons, stickers (Karen Foster); flower (Prima); glitter paper (Doodlebug)

Princess Tania Willis

Layouts for display beg for dimensional texture, both visual and tactile. Ribbons, silk flowers, rhinestones and other dimensional accents really give Cari's layout sensory appeal. Don't be afraid to go lumpy! To make your layout easier to display, back it with chipboard and use a plate holder to hold it in place. And if you're worried about grubby fingers and dust, simply insert the layout into a page protector before displaying.

"Flat"tering Displays
Ways to show off your flat layouts

- Clip a layout on a clipboard.

- Slide a layout under ribbons in a French bulletin board.

- Put a layout in an acrylic frame.

- Prop up a layout using a specimen stand.

- Designate a frame as the "rotating layout" frame. Let it stand in one place, but change the layouts regularly.

- Turn your refrigerator into an art gallery for layouts.

- Put layouts in simple black frames and hang them down a long hallway, gallery style.

- Create a decorative border in a room using layouts instead of using a wallpaper border.

Patterned Paper

Those Eyes *Cari Fennell*

Supplies: Patterned paper, transparency (Hambly); flower, rhinestones, rub-on letters, sticker, transparent letters (Heidi Swapp); ribbon (BasicGrey, Fancy Pants); toulle; chipboard heart (Li'l Davis); stamp (Fancy Pants); acrylic paint; ink; pen

For a Baby Girl Suzy Plantamura

Oh, baby! This gift set sure is cute. Suzy converted a plain wooden box into an adorable storage container just perfect for small toys or other baby gear. All it took was some paint, patterned paper and a few embellishments to create a darling, yet functional baby gift. With the leftover supplies, Suzy made a picture-perfect frame that is perfectly coordinated. Now all Suzy needs is for one of her friends to have a baby!

Wooden Box and Frame

Supplies: Toy box (Sierra Pacific Crafts); frame (unknown); chipboard, patterned paper, stickers, tags (Creative Imaginations); safety pin (Li'l Davis); green rickrack (Making Memories); flower ribbon, picket fence, pink rickrack (unknown); paint

Sugar and spice and everything nice…and pink! Nothing says "girl" more than splashes of that soft, sweet hue. Christine created this ultra-girly frame to show off a photo of her daughter. What began life as an undressed frame with a simple snapshot was transformed into a personalized flower and fairy-clad fantasy her daugher is sure to adore. Well-placed rub-ons, ribbons in bows, colorful stickers and whimsical patterned paper bring this boring border to life. And the photos comes to life too! Adorably decorated frames not only enhance a room's decor but they also enhance the framed photo too. Note how your eyes are drawn to this sweet girl's smile—one that will surely light up the room. This frame would make any little girl feel like a pretty princess!

Frame

Ry Christine Traversa

Supplies: Frame (Hobby Lobby); cardstock; die-cut stickers, patterned paper, rub-on letters (Reminisce); crocheted flower (Studio Calico); button (Autumn Leaves); rub-ons (American Crafts); ribbon (May Arts); adhesive foam; ink

Kids grow up so fast. If you blink, there goes another year. But you can stop time in its tracks with a mini-album like Greta's that celebrates her child's journey through age three. Each age is precious and worth documenting. And this adorable chipboard album is the perfect way to capture any moment before it fades away. All it takes is a few supplies, a little time, and a dash of creative inspiration.

Chipboard Mini Album

Supplies: Chipboard album, ribbon (Maya Road); patterned paper (Scenic Route); chipboard letters and shapes (Maya Road, Scenic Route); letter stickers (Making Memories); rhinestones; flowers (Bazzill, Prima); rub-ons (American Crafts, Scenic Route); digital frames by Rhonna Farrer (Two Peas in a Bucket)

Celebrate Three Greta Hammond

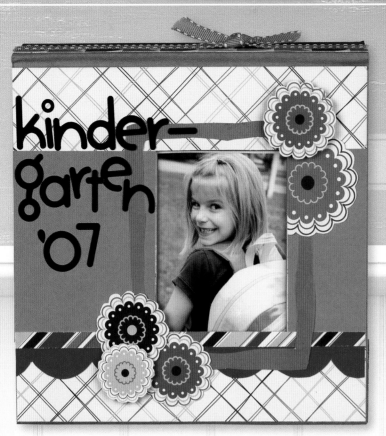

Sometimes we get caught in artistic ruts simply because we do what is accepted as the "norm." Part of memory art is about looking at things differently. Even a small change can make a difference. Take Courtney's album, for instance. Instead of having the binding on the left (as is the usual configuration) she put her binding on top and oriented all the pages accordingly. This transformed her album to a flip format, which makes it both unique and easy to display.

Supplies: Album (Westrim); patterned paper (American Crafts); letter stickers (Doodlebug, KI Memories); stickers (Making Memories); chipboard flowers (Around The Block); quote sticker (KI Memories); ribbon (unknown); Century Gothic font (Microsoft)

Kindergarten Courtney Walsh

Chipboard Mini Album

Chipboard is a scrapbooker's best friend, whether it's used for layouts or albums. This versatile material comes in so many shapes, sizes and products that it makes it sometimes difficult to choose what to use! Cari picked a tiny chipboard kit as the base for her vibrant mini book. She added photos, patterned paper and some decorating whiz to create a miniature memory keeper that still makes a big statement.

Torrey created this photo block puzzle to sit proudly on a coffee or game table. With six sides on each cube, she was able to create six different puzzles. She laminated the photos before adhering them to the blocks, and she coated the sides without photos with acrylic sealant to ensure durability and easy clean-up should chocolate-covered fingers come to play.

Wooden Cubes

Sisters Torrey Scott

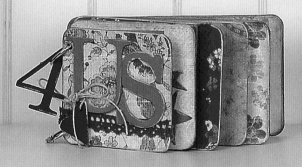

Us Cari Fennell

Supplies: Wooden cubes (unknown); patterned paper (SEI); chipboard letters (K&Co.); stickers (EK Success); typewriter letter slides (Paper Studio); ribbon slide (Making Memories); ribbon (Offray); laminate machine (Xyron); chipboard; cloth bookbinding tape

Photos by Kelli Noto, Dian Carville and Wayne Diggs

Supplies: Chipboard album, letters and shapes, patterned paper, stamps (Fancy Pants); ribbon (Fancy Pants, Scenic Route); rhinestones (Heidi Swapp); paint; decorative punch; buttons (Autumn Leaves); notebook paper; staples; hole punch; ink; pen

Here's to the middle child! They aren't the oldest, they aren't the baby. They are caught in the invisible middle…until now. Nic decided it was high time to showcase this oft-overlooked topic. She chose thick acrylic sheets to create the pages of her album. Using acrylic as an album base makes for a durable foundation that will last for years. Plus, it's an interesting alternative to chipboard or cardstock.

Supplies: Acrylic sheets (from local glass merchant); cardstock; patterned paper (My Mind's Eye); letter stickers (Adornit, Scenic Route); chipboard letters (Heidi Swapp); chipboard accents (American Crafts, Collections); felt arrows (American Crafts); ribbon (Maya Road); stamp (7gypsies, Autumn Leaves); photo turns (7gypsies); pen

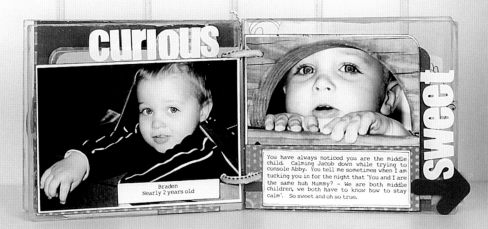

Middle Child Nic Howard

Walks along the beach and sand between your toes: These are the moments we want to relive. With a vacation album like Cari's, you can revisit them anytime. Cari used printed transparencies to create the album pages. And by using black-and-white photos, the pictures don't compete with the bright colors of the album. To complete the display, she re-purposed and decorated a metal tin.

Clearly Unique
The art (and challenge) of the transparent album

- If using acrylic sheets, use a high-speed drill to make holes for binding rings, and don't forget to sand the edges.

- Try using pink tacky tape to adhere elements to an acrylic surface.

- Don't forget to pay attention to both sides of pages since elements will show through from the back.

- Use plain transparencies as pages instead of acrylic sheets to cut down on weight.

- Don't forget about printed transparencies as an option for pages.

Transparencies

Supplies: Tin, flowers (Prima); patterned paper, transparencies (Hambly); letter stamps (Technique Tuesday); heart and butterfly accents, rhinestones (Heidi Swapp); brads (K&Co.); ribbon (May Arts); spray paint; ink

Escape Cari Fennel

Love is said to be circular—it has no beginning and no end. So, how fitting is the circular shape of Christine's love-themed mini album? We often forget that there are other shapes out there besides square and rectangular when it comes to making an album. Don't be afraid to try your hand at round or free-form shaped albums. These often turn out to be the most interesting!

Chipboard Mini Album

Scrapbooking isn't just about paper. New products allow us to combine paper with innovative materials, like acrylic. Vicki employed acrylic as the base for her durable, yet engaging little book. It's bright, colorful and kid-friendly, encouraging little hands to come and play.

Acrylic Mini Album

You Are My Family Vicki Boutin

Supplies: Acrylic album (Pageframe); patterned paper, rub-ons, sticker accents (Daisy D's); letter stickers (Heidi Grace); buttons (Autumn Leaves); rhinestones; ribbon (Offray); pen

Love Christine Traversa

Supplies: Album (Creative Imaginations); cardstock; patterned paper (Imagination Project, SEI); chipboard letters (Li'l Davis); crochet flower (Studio Calico); button (Autumn Leaves); rub-ons (7gypsies, American Crafts, Heidi Swapp); ribbon (Strano, unknown); Century Gothic font (Microsoft)

Cardstock

Sometimes we want albums we can lay on a surface. Sometimes we want albums that can stand on their own. Can one album do both? Yes! That's the beauty of an accordion-fold album. It can be displayed closed, like a book, or it can be placed open on a surface to really entice people to come take a look! Courtney included lots of journaling to read, and added a twist with tags tucked inside little pockets. The creative addition encourages people to come even closer to peek at what's inside.

Supplies: Papers and embellishments (Chatterbox); floss; Arial font (Microsoft)

Like Family Courtney Walsh

Show me how! Making an Accordion Album with Pockets

You will need | *5 sheets of double-sided cardstock, paper trimmer, bone folder, corner rounder (optional), adhesive, circle punch, ribbon, tags or cardstock and a hole punch*

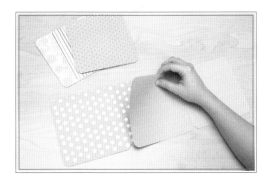

Cut five sheets of 12" x 12" (30cm x 30cm) cardstock down to 6" x 12" (15cm x 30cm). Fold the five sheets in half (to create squares), using a bone folder to set the crease. Round the corners if desired. Unfold the cardstock. Then overlap the left half of one sheet of cardstock on top of the right half of another sheet. Attach the overlapped halves.

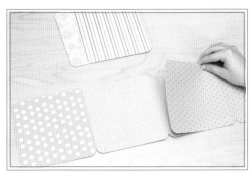

Next, attach the overlapped sheets of cardstock to a third sheet. To do so, overlap the left half of the new sheet of cardstock on top of the right side of the other two sheets. Attach the overlapping pieces, but this time only adhere the bottom edge and two sides (leaving the top open to create a pocket). Continue in this manner to attach the other two sheets of cardstock.

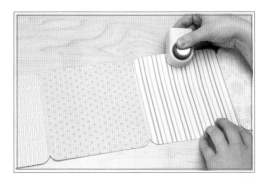

Open up the album so that you can see all six pages. These are the inside pages. Using a circle punch, punch a semi-circle into the top edge of the third, fourth and fifth pages. Make sure to punch only the top sheet of cardstock.

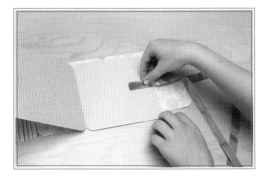

Cut two 9" (23cm) lengths of ribbon. Attach a piece of ribbon to the front and back covers. Then decorate your pages and slip tags into the pockets. You can use pre-made tags or make them by punching a hole in a small cardstock rectangle. To complete, fold the album into an accordian.

Some embellishments are impractical to include on a layout. Kathleen loved this little doorknob and knew the only way she could use it would be outside the album. She dressed this house-shaped mini book with a homey theme, allowing her the perfect place to put her treasured element.

Chipboard Album

We predict you'll love this cute indoor birdhouse—after all, it's in the cards. Vanessa made this adorable little birdhouse out of, you guessed it, playing cards. And, just like birds building a nest, all it took were bits and pieces and odds and ends of rickrack, paper and buttons and what-nots to create this nifty house fit for any niche.

Oversized Playing Cards

Supplies: Playing cards (Heidi Swapp); buttons, chipboard sign, patterned paper (Autumn Leaves); felt flowers (American Crafts, KI Memories); rub-ons (BasicGrey); hinges (Making Memories); brads (Junkitz); felt (Hobby Lobby); ribbon (Michaels); rickrack (Wrights)

Home Tweet Home Vanessa Hudson   **Our Home** Kathleen Summers

Supplies: Album, door knob accent (7gypsies); patterned paper (BasicGrey, My Mind's Eye); stamps (Inque Boutique); ink; embossing powder

Mini albums aren't just for laying out on a table or shelf. Vanessa affixed hers to quilted fabric and framed it to create a warm and cozy display that's as welcoming as it is beautiful. She used a house-shaped chipboard album as the base for her mini album. After she decorated her album with patterned paper, stamps and embellishments, she glued it to the fabric background and framed it with an antique-looking frame sans glass.

Frame and Chipboard Mini Album

Our Home Vanessa Hudson

Supplies: Chipboard album (Maya Road); fabric, frame (Hobby Lobby); chipboard letters, flower, metal corner, patterned paper, stickers (K&Co.); stamps (Autumn Leaves); ribbon (Making Memories); ink

It's clear this album is different. Why? Look closely and you'll see—everything! Jodi made her album pages out of transparency film. This is challenging because both sides of a page are visible. It takes a bit of planning to place all the elements, but the effect is clearly stunning!

Transparent Mini Album

Toasters, serving dishes and wine glasses. These are what couples can as wedding gifts. Forget the wedding registry. Those were made for people who aren't creative! Jodi created a keepsake frame for a happy couple using their wedding colors. A frame like this is the perfect place for photos of a couple's special day.

Collage Frame

Love Jodi Amidei

Happy Together Jodi Amidei

Supplies: Frame (unknown); patterned paper (Creative Imaginations); stamps (Autumn Leaves, Hampton Arts, Scrappy Cat); ribbon (Hobby Lobby, Michaels); paper flowers (Creative Co-op); glitter pen; ink

Supplies: Mini album (unknown); fabric paper (Michael Miller); mesh (Cardauex Trimmings); ribbon (May Arts, Offray); buttons (Jesse James); plastic corners (Close To My Heart, Jesse James); transparency; acrylic paint; embossing template (Provo Craft)

Here's another fun version of an acrylic album. These unique albums are quickly becoming a fun, and sturdy alternative to traditional mini album platforms. Sandi created a travel album, storybook style, where her photos tell the story of a favorite family vacation. She used lots of bold patterns and colors to further the sense of fun and frolic. Travel albums are a great way to preserve and show off the memories of your trips.

Supplies: Acrylic album (Art Bar); cardstock; cardstock stickers, patterned paper, tags, twill (Creative Imaginations); letter stickers (BasicGrey); chipboard letters and shapes, rhinestones, tabs (Heidi Swapp); date stamp (Making Memories); rub-ons (Heidi Swapp, Making Memories); dimensional paint; rub-on letters (Imagination Project)

Bound Together
Materials for binding homemade mini albums

- Loose binder ring
- Stitching (either hand or machine)
- Yarn or string
- Staples
- Bulldog or binder clips
- Cloth bookbinding material
- Ribbon or twill
- Spiral or wire binding

A Good Life Sandi Minchuk

The longer you scrapbook the more you tend to look at objects around you and see potential for projects everywhere. Kathleen's carousel album is a perfect example of this. With some basic supplies, she transformed this ribbon spool into a unique tabletop album that can be adapted for any theme. She attached the pages to the spool's core using ribbon that she adhered length-wise to the pages and then to the spool. Genius!

Garden Carousel Kathleen Summers

Supplies: Ribbon spool, flower ribbon, paper flowers (Prima); patterned paper (Fancy Pants); stamps (Inque Boutique); striped ribbon (unknown); rhinestones

Ribbon Spool

Many of us have pictures lining our office shelves, home desks and mantels. Why not replace those with a layout instead? Layouts can go anywhere! All it takes is a stand to display it on. Whether it's a pre-made wooden stand like this one or one made from folded chipboard, displaying your layouts is a great way to jazz up and personalize your surroundings.

Patterned Paper

Supplies: Patterned paper, chipboard letters and leaves, journaling card, stamps (Fancy Pants); acrylic paint; flowers (Prima); rhinestones; buttons (Autumn Leaves, vintage); ink; pen

XOXO Cari Fennell

Zipper Album

You don't always need to be an open book. Sometimes it makes sense to use an album with a closure, like this zippered case. Closures create intrigue and wonder and provide a cozy place for housing photos. Plus, zippered albums are great for storing loose memorabilia, tiny trinkets or small travel souvenirs. Take a cue from Cari and zip it!

Supplies: Cardstock, zipper album (Bazzill); cardstock accents, chipboard, patterned paper, stamps (Fancy Pants); flowers (Heidi Swapp, Prima); ribbon (May Arts); clip (7gypsies); flower brad, letter sticker (Making Memories); hearts, journal spots, rhinestones (Heidi Swapp); beads (Queen & Co.); ink; pins (Heidi Grace); buttons (Autumn Leaves); notebook paper; staples; envelope twine

F Cari Fennell

Laminated Paper

Family Catherine Feegel-Erhardt

It's a layout. It's a tote bag. It's portable memory art! Now you really can take it with you! Catherine designed this tote bag using laminated color copies of two scrapbook layouts and some extra patterned paper. She punched holes in all the sides and laced them all together with yarn. For the handle, she took clear hardware store tubing and stuffed it with bits of colored yarn. Then she attached the handles to the tote through grommets using binder rings. It's art on the go!

Supplies (to make layout): Cardstock; patterned paper (BasicGrey); chipboard flowers (EK Success); chipboard letters (Everlasting Keepsakes); fibers (BasicGrey); brads; photo turns; adhesive foam; ink; pen

Supplies (to make bag): Yarn; grommets (Prym); clear tubing (hardware store); binder rings; laminating machine (Kinkos)

Amy created this accordion album for her father-in-law's 60th birthday. It's a beautiful and loving tribute chock-full of photos and memories throughout his life. But the best part is the back of the album serves as the guest book where people signed and left their well-wishes. This would be a great heart-felt project for any celebration!

Leather Box and Cardstock

Look Who's 60 Amy Peterman

Supplies: Leather box (unknown); cardstock; chipboard letters, patterned paper, ribbon, rub-ons, stamps (Fancy Pants); decorative tape (7gypsies); letter stickers (Making Memories); acrylic paint; brads; staples; ink; pen

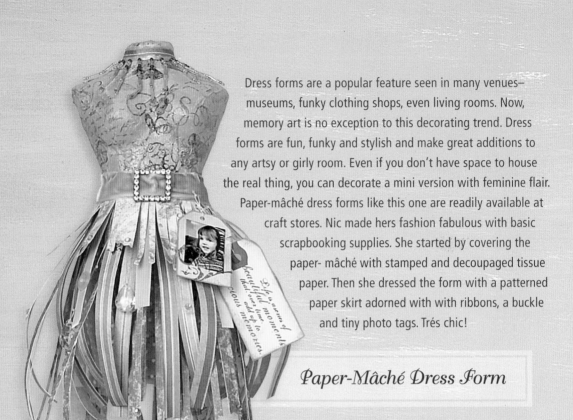

Dress forms are a popular feature seen in many venues—museums, funky clothing shops, even living rooms. Now, memory art is no exception to this decorating trend. Dress forms are fun, funky and stylish and make great additions to any artsy or girly room. Even if you don't have space to house the real thing, you can decorate a mini version with feminine flair. Paper-mâché dress forms like this one are readily available at craft stores. Nic made hers fashion fabulous with basic scrapbooking supplies. She started by covering the paper-mâché with stamped and decoupaged tissue paper. Then she dressed the form with a patterned paper skirt adorned with with ribbons, a buckle and tiny photo tags. Trés chic!

Paper-Mâché Dress Form

Precious Memories Nic Howard

Supplies: Paper-mâché dress form (unknown); patterned paper, rub-ons (Fancy Pants); stamps (Fancy Pants, Oxford, PSX, Stamp in the Hand); ink; tissue paper; trim (Making Memories); fabric (Tarisota); heart pins (Heidi Grace); jewels (Heidi Swapp); rhinestone accent (Delish Designs); paint; decoupage medium; varnish

Original project idea from Wendy Redshaw-Bruhns

Show me how! Decorating Paper-Mâché with Tissue Paper

You will need | *rubber stamp, solvent ink in a dark color, white tissue paper, paper-mâché object, brush, decoupage medium, acrylic paint, water, satin varnish*

Stamp designs on several sheets of white tissue paper using solvent ink. Then tear the tissue paper into short, wide strips.

Brush the back of a strip of tissue paper with decoupage medium and adhere it to the paper-mâché. Continue layering strips until the paper-mâché is covered completely with tissue paper.

Apply decoupage medium over the top of the tissue paper, smoothing out the application where needed.

Thin the acrylic paint with water. Then brush the paint over the tissue paper. When the paint dries, brush a layer of satin varnish over the entire piece.

Artist trading cards (ATCs) have really come into their own as an art form. They are perfect mini projects for scrapbookers and they allow us to share our craft with each other! The trouble is, what do we do with all the ATCs we collect? It seems a shame to dump them in a box. Torrey created this beautiful mini version of a star book to hold all her ATCs. There are several designs for star books available out there, and most can be pared down to a smaller size. Give it a try!

Supplies: Patterned paper (Chatterbox, Design Originals, K&Co., Scenic Route); chipboard letters (K&Co.); Braille paper (unknown); ribbon (K&Co., Offray, Stampin' Up); rhinestones; stamps (Autumn Leaves, Heidi Swapp, Hero Arts, Inkadinkado); flowers (Prima); ink

atc Torrey Scott

We all have our little fetishes, secret obsessions or clandestine collections. Being artists, we tend to hold on to all sorts of "treasures" that most people would simply dismiss as trash. Silly people. They don't know what they're missing! But you do. Follow Genevieve's lead and turn your little treasures into memory art. Genevieve admits that she has an affinity for collecting boxes. After years of allowing it to collect dust, she decided to spiff up this cute little wooden box and give it a new face and a new purpose—whatever that may be! Don't forget that memory art isn't limited to basic scrapbooking supplies. Fabric, sequins and gold accents stored around the house really spice up a piece and add a unique flair to things that are square. So, go ahead and bring your own hidden treasures out into the open and turn them into memory art gold.

Wooden Box

Supplies: Box (unknown); fabric (Amy Butler); rub-ons (7gypsies, Chatterbox); paint; ribbon, sequins (unknown)

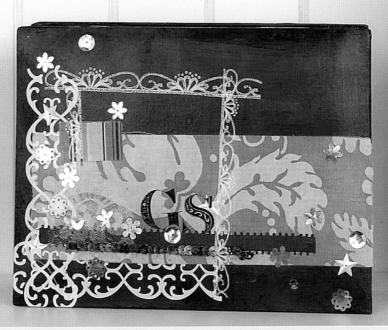

Funky Genevieve Simmonds

Paper-Mâché Box

Use As Directed *Tiffany Tillman*

When you visit someone's home, it's always a nice surprise to find a little something sweet sitting in a candy dish. It's an even nicer surprise when the candy comes in a beautifully hand-decorated box. Tiffany loves making small decorative pieces out of her scrapbook supply scraps. With a few odds and ends of paper, ribbons, paint and embellishments, she created this bright and cheerful candy box that's sure to perk up any room.

Supplies: Box (Michaels); patterned paper (BasicGrey); ribbon (Fancy Pants); brad button (K&Co.); tag (Heidi Swapp); acrylic paint

Metal Bin

Our Kids *Catherine Feegel-Erhardt*

When we artists look around our houses, nothing escapes our scrutiny. The thing about memory art is that we can take any household object and transform it into a thing of beauty, even a plain metal bin. Catherine decorated this metal container with pretty papers and a printed transparency before she added a favorite photo and ribbon. The result is a receptacle that will bring joy to whatever purpose it's designated for.

Supplies: Metal bin (unknown); patterned paper (Creative Imaginations, Scenic Route); transparency (Hambly); ribbon (Making Memories, Michaels, Offray, unknown); acrylic paint; adhesive foam

Chipboard albums are so versatile! Some patterned paper and aptly chosen embellishments can transform them for any theme. Suzy chose to make her chipboard album into something soft and feminine for her sister's new family. But using bright, cheery patterns would make the perfect album for a little boy's birthday or a day at the beach. Plus, chipboard albums' small size make them a great first project for new memory artists.

Supplies: Patterned paper (Crate Paper, Die Cuts With A View); buttons (Autumn Leaves); ink; flowers (Prima); ribbon, rickrack (Me & My Big Ideas, unknown); chipboard letters (American Crafts, Crate Paper, Heidi Swapp); flowers, velvet flower ribbon (Maya Road); rub-ons (Adornit, Crate Paper, Fancy Pants, K&Co., My Mind's Eye)

Elliott Family Suzy Plantamura

Chipboard House Kit

Do you remember playing dress-up and dolls? Seems like a lifetime ago. Even if you own your own home, you're never too old to play house! Vicki constructed this whimsical fold-out house album from a blank chipboard kit. By decorating it with paper, rhinestones, buttons, rub-ons and other embellishments she made this tiny house and its photos come alive. Follow Vicki's creative lead and make your own little home to display. Dress the kit in travel stickers and "house" your vacation pictures. Tell the story of your childhood accompanied by favorite vintage photos. Decorate the tiny walls in hues of red and green to create an adorable gingerbread house for the holidays. With a little inspiration and lots of imagination you can turn this little house into a home for any theme.

Devyn's House Vicki Boutin

Supplies: Chipboard house kit, letter stickers, patterned paper (Crafty Secrets); stamps (Gel a tins); flower (Li'l Davis); buttons (Autumn Leaves); rub-ons (Royal & Langnickel); glitter; rhinestones; ribbon (unknown); ink

Sending flowers is a nice way to show someone you care. Making flowers is even better! Sandi used premade chipboard flowers as templates for her cut-out paper flowers. She attached the flowers to wooden skewers then inserted them into clay in the bottom of a metal bin she also decorated with paper. She loosely packed in Spanish moss to add a finished look to her arrangement. The best thing about these flowers is you never have to water them, and they won't ever wilt!

Cardstock and Metal Bin

For You Sandi Minchuk

Supplies: Bin (Target); cardstock; patterned paper (Die Cuts With A View); buttons (Autumn Leaves, Die Cuts With A View); chipboard flowers used as templates (Everlasting Keepsakes, Fancy Pants, Magistical Memories, Maya Road, Pressed Petals); moss; florist's tape; wooden skewers; clay

Memory art isn't always about displaying photos. Sometimes it's just about creating something daringly bold and beautiful just for art's sake. Genevieve took a trip to the hardware store to find the plywood for her display frame. By mixing textures, colors, media and products she created this fun and funky display board designed to hold cards and photos. Experimenting is fun and freeing for that muse that sits patiently in us all. So let her rip! Pull out the conventional stops and try creating just because.

Supplies: Plywood (Home Depot); cardstock; fabric (Amy Butler); fabric paper (KI Memories); word stickers (Die Cuts With A View); letters (Heidi Swapp); stamps (Purple Onion); ink; gesso; rub-ons (BasicGrey, Fontwerks, Hambly); binder clip; staples

Plywood

For Dad Genevieve Simmonds

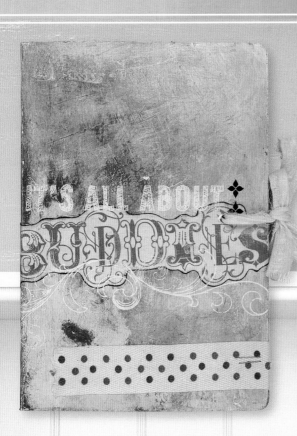

Children's Board Book

A Note About Albums

- Repurpose notebooks, journals, children's board books or paper sacks to create interesting albums.

- In cardstock albums, reinforce binding holes to prevent tear through.

- To prevent dirt and damage, store albums in a decorated box.

- Albums can be displayed anywhere! Try opening one on a coffee table, stacking it on a shelf, or hanging it from a doorknob or hook.

In school, the "three Rs" are reading, writing and 'rithmetic. In scrapbooking they are recycle, repurpose and reuse. Genevieve took a children's board book and applied the three Rs. The result is this rustic-looking mini album. Genevieve likes making mini albums because it allows her to use several photos, even the "not so good" ones. She reminds us that every photo can tell a story and has the potential to be displayed.

Supplies: Board book (unknown); patterned paper (Creative Imaginations); rub-ons (7gypsies, Autumn Leaves, BasicGrey, Daisy D's, Fontwerks); die-cut title (My Mind's Eye); twill (Autumn Leaves); stamp (7gypsies); paint; pen

Wooden Cubes

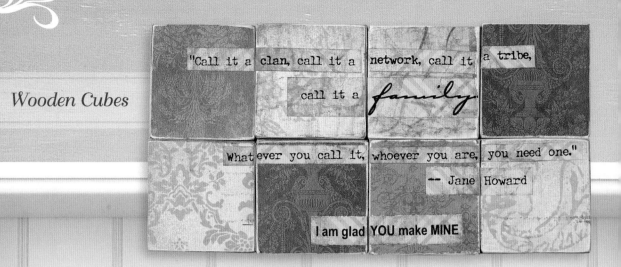

Art is at its best when it can be enjoyed by more than just the eyes. This decorated cube puzzle has beautifully subtle colors that give it a sophisticated feel. It also provides a tactile experience for those enjoying the look. Who doesn't crave to solve a puzzle put before them? And with your imagination and your store of scrapping supplies, think of all the puzzles you can create! Bold, bright and playful or soft and sophisticated. Family time, fun time or your favorite foods. The possibilities are endless! Try Mou's design (see right) and adorn your cubes with a variety of supplies: rub-ons and chipboard, photos and sanded paper. Or stick to making photo cubes. And don't forget the carryall. Decorate a box or tray to match your puzzle. It will not only corral your cubes but provide a pleasing place for display. Above all, when creating a beautiful project to put around the house, don't forget to look at how it can be pretty as well as interactive.

Supplies: Wooden tray (Darice); wooden cubes (Michaels); patterned paper (Colorbok, Die Cuts With A View); chipboard letters (Zsiage); letter accents (Colorbok); rub-on word (Deja Views); acrylic paint; ink; decoupage medium; Arial Narrow, Carpenter, Typewriter fonts (Microsoft)

U R Mine Mou Saha

Show me how! Making a Cube Puzzle

You will need | *wooden cubes, pencil, patterned paper, photos, scissors or paper trimmer, decoupage medium, sandpaper (optional), rub-ons, chipboard, box or tray*

Line up your cubes as they will be placed in a tray or box. Use pencil or chalk to note what materials will be placed on each side of the cubes. Be sure to rotate the cubes in the same direction so that when the cubes are displayed, quotes, words and photos are oriented correctly.

Gather patterned paper and print out photos. Cut the paper and photos into 2" (5cm) squares. You will need six squares for each cube.

Attach the paper and photos to the cubes using decoupage medium. Make sure all the edges and corners are tacked down. If desired, sand the edges of the cubes to create a soft look.

Add embellishments, like rub-ons and chipboard letters, to the cubes. Decorate your box or tray to match the cubes.

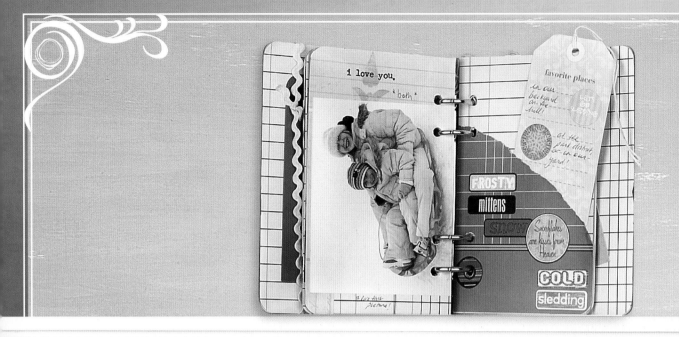

Clean lines, black-and-white photos, uncluttered layouts and just the right splash of red; all these spell out the look we have come to know (and love) as graphic. By maintaining the graphic look from cover to cover, Tiffany created a stylish mini album that will be a striking addition to her home décor. Keeping things simple doesn't mean they have to be plain. The graphic look is sophisticated and proves, once again, that less is more.

Supplies: Album (Heidi Swapp); cardstock; patterned paper (BasicGrey, Scenic Route); rub-ons (Hambly, KI Memories, Urban Lily); letters (American Crafts, Heidi Swapp); flowers (Queen & Co.); brads; ribbon (Strano); Teletype font (Internet download)

Chipboard Mini Album

Make Memories Tiffany Tillman

School's in session—memory art school that is—so make sure you have all the supplies you'll need. First on the list is a notebook. But not for taking notes. It's for altering into something wonderful, meaningful and just plain fun! Christine transformed this unassuming three-ring notebook album into an adorable mini book filled with memories. Creating a notebook mini album is one homework assignment you won't mind completing.

Chipboard Mini Album

Memories *Christine Traversa*

Supplies: Album (Creative Imaginations); patterned paper (Creative Imaginations, Jenni Bowlin); letter stickers (Heidi Swapp); crochet flower (Studio Calico); button (Autumn Leaves); tags (Making Memories, Martha Stewart); ribbon; sticker accents (Reminisce); pen

Chipboard Mini Album

Who says Christmas has to be about snow-covered trees, sleigh rides and cocoa by the fire? Holidays are to be celebrated (and commemorated) any way we choose! Gretchen made her chipboard mini album look like a traditional holiday book on the outside, but open it up and find a Christmas celebration as a trip to Disney World. What a fun way to memorialize a holiday get together! Gretchen brought the storybook theme inside the album with "Once Upon a Time," while Christmas-colored tabs guide readers to the right spot.

Supplies: Album (Maya Road); patterned paper (Scrapworks); stamps (Autumn Leaves, Fontwerks); chipboard letters, decorative tape, rub-ons, stars (Heidi Swapp); letter stickers (Making Memories); chipboard (Scenic Route); notebook paper; pen

A Christmas Story Gretchen McElveen

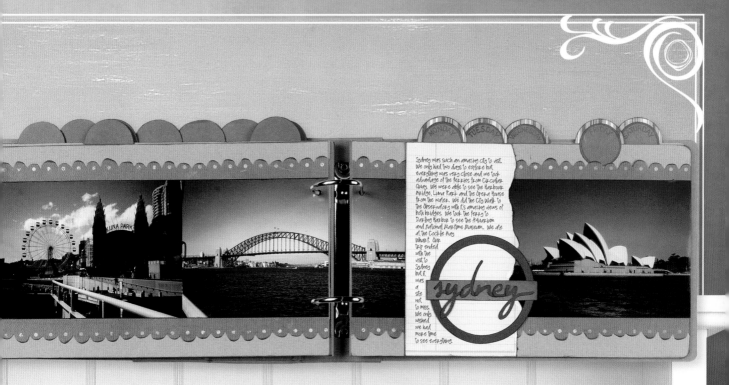

Most of us are guilty of squirreling away photos from a special event, celebration or vacation until we come up with something spectacular to do with them. What a waste! Cindy did this very thing with photos from a once-in-a-lifetime trip. Then one day she decided to unbox the photos and turn them into a simple but lovely travel album that she can enjoy daily. So, what are you waiting for?

Chipboard Mini Album

Supplies: Album, acrylic title letters, metal accent (Making Memories); cardstock; patterned paper (Crate Paper, Making Memories); stamps (Purple Onion); circle template, die-cut shapes (Provo Craft); ink; buttons (SEI); SP Wonderful Way font (Scrap Supply)

One Amazing Trip Cindy Smith

Chipboard Accordian Album

Sometimes, the shape of an album calls for a specific theme. And sometimes your photos guide the project. In these cases, imagination goes a long way in creating memorable memory art. Samantha didn't have fairy princess pictures to adorn her castle album, but she did have photos from the beach. So she took a creative approach and dressed this mini book in a sandy theme. Adorable action photos, strips of patterned paper, handwritten journaling and some colorful accents all lend a bit of fun to this album about beach babes. (Samantha's tip: To prevent the edges of patterned paper from peeling up off the chipboard, run them through an adhesive application machine.) Samantha's project reminds us to stick to the heart of our craft: If you're not having fun with your memory art, you're not doing something right!

Beach Babe Samantha Walker

Supplies: Album, chipboard letters, patterned paper, rub-ons, sticker accents (Creative Imaginations); cardstock; Kraft cardstock; ink; pen

Catherine wanted a fun way to document the comings and goings of friends at her beach cottage, so she crafted an inviting guest book to do just that. She decorated each page with patterned paper, stamped images, stickers and fibers to create a beautiful, fun-in-the-sun mini book that's just begs to be filled with notes and well wishes. Raffia and seashells lend the perfect beachy feel to the book. In fact, if you hold it up to your ear, you can almost hear the sound of the surf.

Supplies: Patterned paper (7gypsies, BasicGrey, EK Success, Karen Foster, Reminisce, Rusty Pickle, Stamping Station, Wube); transparencies (Creative Imaginations, Hambly); letters (Heidi Swapp); rhinestones; ribbon (American Crafts, Berwick, May Arts, Offray); shells; stamp (Catslife, Heidi Swapp); ink; paint; thread; binder rings; tabs; raffia; tag

Beach Guests Catherine Feegel-Erhardt

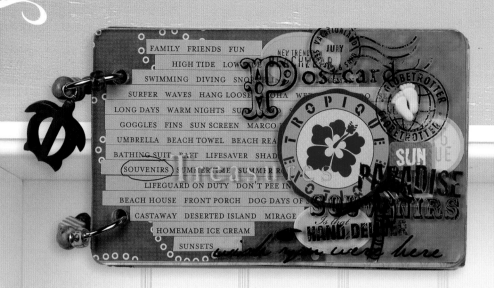

Cardstock and Acrylic Album Covers

It's not surprising that travel albums are a popular form of memory art. With so many photos and fun memories to record from a trip, mini books are a great way to get some pictures in an album and show off fun times. But travel albums don't have to mean photo albums. What about your pile of postcards, museum ticket stubs or hotel stationery? Don't forget to include these in your albums along with–or instead of–photos. A little journaling and some fun embellishments can tell a story just as well as photos. Travel themed rub-ons are a fun way to dress up the acrylic covers of a vacation souvenir album. The rub-ons add just the right amount of color and whimsy while allowing the inside pages to peek through. Mou used bits and pieces of scrap rub-on sheets for her album covers. After decorating, just bind the pages with some rings, add fun dimensional souvenirs and your travel album will be ready to explore.

Paradise Souvenirs Mou Saha

Supplies: Album (D.Reeves Design House); patterned paper, rub-ons (Frances Meyer); stickers (7gypsies, Frances Meyer); metal tabs (Making Memories); hole punch; pen

Show me how! Making a Souvenir Album

You will need | acrylic album covers, rub-ons, patterned cardstock, corner rounder, scissors or paper trimmer, hole punch, postcards, stickers, souvenirs, 2 binder rings, beads and other dimensional accents

On the album front cover, rub on various words and designs that match the album's theme. Add one rub-on at a time.

Cut 10 or more 4" x 6.5" (10cm x 17cm) pieces of patterned cardstock. Round the papers' corners.

Use the album cover as a template to mark holes in the cardstock pieces for the binder rings. Punch the holes using a ⅛" hole punch.

Attach souvenir postcards to several of the pages. Add souvenirs, stickers and journaling to other pages. When the pages are complete, stack them with the covers and thread binder rings through the holes. Add beads, charms and other dimensional accents to the binder rings before closing them.

Not all shadow boxes are created equally. In fact, some aren't even shadow boxes at all! Courtney didn't have the heart to throw away this case from one of her son's toys. Instead, she altered it into a cool shadowbox display for her husband's office. Courtney wanted to preserve some favorite faces of children that her husband, a children's pastor, works with. She even threw in some candy to further her kid-friendly theme.

Metal Case

Supplies: Metal case (MEGA brand toy packaging); chipboard letters (All My Memories); felt flowers (Queen & Co.); ink; digital frame by Rhonna Farrer (Two Peas in a Bucket); Century Gothic font (Microsoft)

Faith Kids Courtney Walsh

Wooden Cubes

Favorite Photos Tania Willis

One aspect of memory art that sets it apart from traditional scrapbooking is that it lends itself well to being interactive. Tania wanted a project that would appeal to her children, and would be durable enough to withstand lots of handling. She created these fun and colorful photo cubes and used a clear acrylic sealer to adhere the photos to the cubes and add a protective coating to the top of the photos. It's important to remember the smallest members of our viewing audience and make projects just for them, too!

Supplies: Wooden cubes (craft store); decoupage medium

Being organized is something we all strive to be, but because it's so tedious, many of us fail miserably. Perhaps if organization had some pizzazz we'd be more apt to actually try it! Samantha came up with a great solution. She combined memory art with a functional desk caddy to create a fun and inviting way to get the job done. You could use memory art to spruce up all sorts of office-related paraphernalia: paper weights, pencil holders, desk pads, calendars. You could even give your stapler a much-needed facelift!

Desk Caddy

Supplies: Desk caddy, chipboard bookplate and flowers, patterned paper, rub-ons, stickers (Creative Imaginations); cardstock; paint; pen

Cherish Good Times Samantha Walker

Source guide

The following companies manufacture products featured in this book. Please check your local retailers to find these materials, or go to a company's Web site for the latest product. In addition, we have made every attempt to properly credit the items mentioned in this book. We apologize to any company that we have listed incorrectly, and we would appreciate hearing from you.

7gypsies
(877) 749-7797
www.sevengypsies.com

AccuCut
(800) 288-1670
www.accucut.com

Adobe Systems Incorporated
(800) 833-6687
www.adobe.com

Adornit/Carolee's Creations
(435) 563-1100
www.adornit.com

All My Memories
(888) 553-1998
www.allmymemories.com

AMACO - American Art Clay Co.
(800) 374-1600
www.amaco.com

American Crafts
(801) 226-0747
www.americancrafts.com

Amy Butler Design
(740) 587-2841
www.amybutlerdesign.com

Anna Griffin, Inc.
(888) 817-8170
www.annagriffin.com

Arctic Frog
(479) 636-3764
www.arcticfrog.com

Around The Block
(801) 593-1946
www.aroundtheblockproducts.com

Art Bar - no source available

Autumn Leaves
(800) 588-6707
www.autumnleaves.com

BAM POP LLC
www.bampop.com

BasicGrey
(801) 544-1116
www.basicgrey.com

Bazzill Basics Paper
(480) 558-8557
www.bazzillbasics.com

Beadery, The
(800) 422-4472
www.thebeadery.com

Berwick Offray, LLC
(800) 344-5533
www.offray.com

Buttons Galore & More
(856) 753-6700
www.buttonsgaloreandmore.com

Cardeaux Trimmings - no source available

Catslife Press
(541) 902-7855
www.harborside.com/~catslife/

Chatterbox, Inc.
(888) 416-6260
www.chatterboxinc.com

Cherry On Top, A
www.acherryontop.com

CherryArte
(212) 465-3495
www.cherryarte.com

Close To My Heart
(888) 655-6552
www.closetomyheart.com

Cloud 9 Design
(866) 348-5661
www.cloud9design.biz

Collage Press
(435) 676-2039
www.collagepress.com

Collections Elements
www.bumblebeecrafts.com.au

Colorbök, Inc.
(800) 366-4660
www.colorbok.com

Cosmo Cricket
(800) 852-8810
www.cosmocricket.com

Craf-T Products
www.craf-tproducts.com

Crafts, Etc. Ltd.
(800) 888-0321 x 1275
www.craftsetc.com

Crafty Secrets Publications
(888) 597-8898
www.craftysecrets.com

Crate Paper
(801) 798-8996
www.cratepaper.com

Creative Co-op
(866) 323-2264
www.creativecoop.com

Creative Imaginations
(800) 942-6487
www.cigift.com

Creative Memories
(800) 468-9335
www.creativememories.com

D.Reeves Design House
www.dreevesdesignhouse.blogspot.com

Daisy D's Paper Company
(888) 601-8955
www.daisydspaper.com

Darice, Inc.
(800) 321-1494
www.darice.com

Déjà Views
(800) 243-8419
www.dejaviews.com

Delish Designs
(360) 897-1254
www.delishdesigns.com

Dennis Daniels
(408) 848-8833
www.dennisdaniels.com

Design Originals
(800) 877-7820
www.d-originals.com

Designer Digitals
www.designerdigitals.com

Die Cuts With A View
(801) 224-6766
www.diecutswithaview.com

Doodlebug Design, Inc.
(877) 800-9190
www.doodlebug.ws

EK Success, Ltd.
(800) 524-1349
www.eksuccess.com

Everlasting Keepsakes
(816) 896-7037
www.everlastingkeepsakes.com

Fancy Pants Designs, LLC
(801) 779-3212
www.fancypantsdesigns.com

FedEx Kinko's
www.fedex.com

FiberMark
(802) 257-0365
www.fibermark.com

Fiskars, Inc.
(866) 348-5661
www.fiskars.com

Flair Designs
(888) 546-9990
www.flairdesignsinc.com

Fontwerks
(604) 942-3105
www.fontwerks.com

Frances Meyer, Inc.
(413) 584-5446
www.francesmeyer.com

Gel-a-tins
(800) 393-2151
www.gelatinstamps.com

Golden Artist Colors, Inc.
(800) 959-6543
www.goldenpaints.com

Hallmark Cards, Inc.
(800) 425-5627
www.hallmark.com

Hambly Studios
(800) 451-3999
www.hamblystudios.com

Hampton Art Stamps, Inc.
(800) 229-1019
www.hamptonart.com

Heidi Grace Designs, Inc.
(866) 348-5661
www.heidigrace.com

Heidi Swapp/Advantus Corporation
(904) 482-0092
www.heidiswapp.com

Hero Arts Rubber Stamps, Inc.
(800) 822-4376
www.heroarts.com

Hobby Lobby Stores, Inc.
www.hobbylobby.com

Home Depot U.S.A., Inc.
www.homedepot.com

Hot Off The Press, Inc.
(800) 227-9595
www.b2b.hotp.com

Imagination Project, Inc.
(888) 477-6532
www.imaginationproject.com

Inkadinkado Rubber Stamps
(800) 523-8452
www.inkadinkado.com

Inque Boutique, Inc.
www.inqueboutique.com

Jen Wilson Designs
www.jenwilsondesigns.com

Jenni Bowlin
www.jennibowlin.com

Jesse James & Co., Inc.
(610) 435-0201
www.jessejamesbutton.com

Jo-Ann Stores
www.joann.com

Junkitz
(732) 792-1108
www.junkitz.com

K&Company
(888) 244-2083
www.kandcompany.com

Kaiser Craft
(630) 618-3044
www.kaisercraft.com.au

Karen Foster Design
(801) 451-9779
www.karenfosterdesign.com

KI Memories
(972) 243-5595
www.kimemories.com

Li'l Davis Designs
(480) 223-0080
www.lildavisdesigns.com

Luxe Designs
(972) 573-2120
www.luxedesigns.com

Magic Mesh
(651) 345-6374
www.magicmesh.com

Magistical Memories
(818) 842-1540
www.magisticalmemories.com

Making Memories
(801) 294-0430
www.makingmemories.com

Martha Stewart Crafts
www.marthastewartcrafts.com

May Arts
(800) 442-3950
www.mayarts.com

Maya Road, LLC
(877) 427-7764
www.mayaroad.com

me & my BiG ideas
(949) 583-2065
www.meandmybigideas.com

MEGA
www.megabloks.com

Melissa Frances/Heart & Home, Inc.
(888) 616-6166
www.melissafrances.com

Mermaid Tears
(310) 569-3345
www.mermaidtears.net

Michael Miller Memories
(646) 230-8862
www.michaelmillermemories.com

Michaels Arts & Crafts
(800) 642-4235
www.michaels.com

Microsoft Corporation
www.microsoft.com

My Mind's Eye, Inc.
(800) 665-5116
www.mymindseye.com

NRN Designs
(888) 678-2734
www.nrndesigns.com

Offray- see Berwick Offray, LLC

Oxford Impressions
www.oxfordimpressions.com

Pageframe Designs
(877) 553-7263
www.scrapbookframe.com

Paper Salon
(800) 627-2648
www.papersalon.com

Paper Studio
(480) 557-5700
www.paperstudio.com

Pebbles Inc.
(801) 235-1520
www.pebblesinc.com

Pottery Barn
(800) 993-4923
www.potterybarn.com

Pressed Petals
(800) 748-4656
www.pressedpetals.com

Prima Marketing, Inc.
(909) 627-5532
www.primamarketinginc.com

Provo Craft
(800) 937-7686
www.provocraft.com

Prym Consumer USA, Inc.
www.dritz.com

PSX Design
www.sierra-enterprises.com/psxmain.html

Purple Onion Designs
www.purpleoniondesigns.com

Queen & Co.
(858) 613-7858
www.queenandcompany.com

Ranger Industries, Inc.
(800) 244-2211
www.rangerink.com

Reminisce Papers
(319) 358-9777
www.shopreminisce.com

Rhonna Designs
www.rhonnadesigns.com

Royal & Langnickel/Royal Brush Mfg.
(800) 247-2211
www.royalbrush.com

Rusty Pickle
(801) 746-1045
www.rustypickle.com

Sassafras Lass
(801) 269-1331
www.sassafraslass.com

Scenic Route Paper Co.
(801) 542-8071
www.scenicroutepaper.com

ScrapArtist
(734) 717-7775
www.scrapartist.com

Scrapbook Graphics
www.scrapbookgraphics.com

Scrappy Cat, LLC
(440) 234-4850
www.scrappycatcreations.com

Scrapsupply
(615) 777-3953
www.scrapsupply.com

Scrapworks, LLC/As You Wish Products, LLC
(801) 363-1010
www.scrapworks.com

SEI, Inc.
(800) 333-3279
www.shopsei.com

Sierra Pacific Crafts
(503) 685-6161
www.sierrapacificcrafts.org

A Stamp in the Hand
(310) 515-4818
www.astampinthehand.com

Stampendous!
(800) 869-0474
www.stampendous.com

Stampin' Up!
(800) 782-6787
www.stampinup.com

Stamping Station
(801) 444-3828
www.stampingstation.com

Staples, Inc.
www.staples.com

Sticker Studio
(888) 244-2083
www.stickerstudio.com

Stix 2 Fantastak
www.stix2fantastak.com

Strano Designs
(508) 454-4615
www.stranodesigns.com

Studio Calico
www.studiocalico.com

Sweetwater
(800) 359-3094
www.sweetwaterscrapbook.com

Target
www.target.com

Tarisota Collections
www.tarisota.com.au

Technique Tuesday, LLC
(503) 644-4073
www.techniquetuesday.com

Trace Industries - no longer in business

Two Peas in a Bucket
(888) 896-7327
www.twopeasinabucket.com

Urban Lily
www.urbanlily.com

Wal-Mart Stores, Inc.
www.walmart.com

We R Memory Keepers, Inc.
(801) 539-5000
www.weronthenet.com

Westrim Crafts
(800) 727-2727
www.westrimcrafts.com

Wilton Industries, Inc.
(800) 794-5866
www.wilton.com

Wordsworth
(877) 280-0934
www.wordsworthstamps.com

Wrights Ribbon Accents
(877) 597-4448
www.wrights.com

I ndex

Flip, Spin & Play

Step-by-step instructions on a variety of techniques show you how
to create engaging, interactive pages that beg to be touched.

ISBN-13: 978-1-59963-018-2
ISBN-10: 1-59963-018-4

paperback
128 pages
Z1679

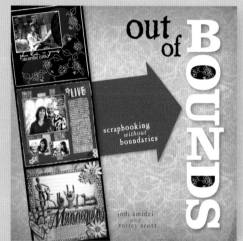

Out of Bounds

Push the boundaries of your
scrapbooking with creative
inspiration and innovative ideas
from leading scrapbook designers
Jodi Amidei and Torrey Scott.

ISBN-13: 978-1-59963-009-0
ISBN-10: 1-59963-009-5

paperback
128 pages
Z0795

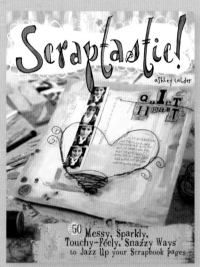

Scraptastic!

Ashley Calder shows you how to experiment with art supplies, try
unfamiliar tools, and have fun making messy, sparkly, touchy-feely,
snazzy scrapbook layouts.

ISBN-13: 978-1-59963-011-3
ISBN-10: 1-59963-011-7

paperback
128 pages
Z1007

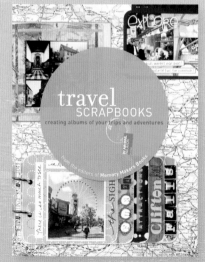

Travel Scrapbooks

Discover creative ways to organize
vacation photos into mini albums
featuring your favorite travel destinations.

ISBN-13: 978-1-59963-008-3
ISBN-10: 1-59963-008-7

paperback
128 pages
Z0789